THE
LONDON
PHILHARMONIC
ORCHESTRA

PHILHARMONIC Jubilee 1932-1982

JERROLD NORTHROP MOORE

A CELEBRATION OF THE LONDON PHILHARMONIC ORCHESTRA'S FIFTIETH ANNIVERSARY

Hutchinson

London Melbourne Sydney Auckland Johannesburg

Chronology

—— **1932** ——
Sir Thomas Beecham forms the London Philharmonic Orchestra; sensational success of debut concert in Queen's Hall.

—— **1933** ——
The first gramophone records are made.

—— **1935** ——
Brussels: the first visit abroad.

—— **1936** ——
Tour of Germany: Hitler, Goebbels, Hess and other Nazi leaders attend the concerts.

—— **1939** ——
Liquidation of the managing company. The Orchestra becomes a players' co-operative, Musical Culture Ltd, and appoints violist Thomas Russell as secretary.

—— **1940** ——
Sir Thomas Beecham goes abroad. J. B. Priestley appeals on the Orchestra's behalf at a 'Musical Manifesto' concert, and Jack Hylton offers the variety theatres for twice-nightly concerts.

—— **1941** ——
Queen's Hall is destroyed by bombing and many of the Orchestra's instruments are lost.

—— **1942** ——
First appearance at the Promenade Concerts, now transferred to the Royal Albert Hall.

—— **1943** ——
The story of the Orchestra's survival against wartime odds is told in a film, *Battle for Music*.

—— **1945** ——
Thomas Russell becomes managing director.

—— **1946** ——
Victor de Sabata and other international conductors work with the Orchestra, ushering in the post-war era.

—— **1947** ——
The London Philharmonic Choir is formed.

—— **1948** ——
Eduard van Beinum appointed principal conductor.

—— **1951** ——
Sir Adrian Boult succeeds van Beinum.

—— **1952** ——
Thomas Russell dismissed because of outside political pressure.

—— **1953** ——
Sir Adrian Boult and the Orchestra complete the recording of Vaughan Williams's symphonies under the composer's supervision.

—— **1956** ——
First visit to the Soviet Union by a British orchestra.

—— **1957** ——
Financial crisis: the players sacrifice fixed incomes, paid holidays and their pension fund.

—— **1958** ——
William Steinberg appointed principal conductor.

—— **1959** ——
Eric Bravington becomes managing director.

—— 1962 ——
First visits by a British orchestra to India, Ceylon, Australia, Hong Kong and the Philippines. John Pritchard appointed principal conductor.

—— 1963 ——
Pablo Casals, at eighty-six, conducts his oratorio, *El Pessebre* (*The Manger*).

—— 1964 ——
First summer as resident orchestra at Glyndebourne Festival Opera.

—— 1965 ——
Sir Adrian Boult accepts the title of president.

—— 1966 ——
Danny Kaye conducts an LPO National Appeal Fund concert.

—— 1967 ——
Bernard Haitink takes up the principal conductorship.

—— 1969 ——
Second tour of the Far East includes first visits to Singapore, Japan and Korea.

—— 1970 ——
First tour in the United States of America.

—— 1971 ——
Tour of Canada, the United States and Mexico.

—— 1972 ——
The Orchestra takes part in the Berlin Festival.

—— 1973 ——
Eric Bravington appointed OBE. Ten concerts at the first Hong Kong Arts Festival. First tour of China by a Western orchestra.

—— 1975 ——
Henry Wood Hall opened as a permanent rehearsal centre. Second Russian tour.

—— 1976 ——
Bicentennial tour of the United States.

—— 1977 ——
Bernard Haitink created honorary KBE. The Queen attends a London Philharmonic concert.

—— 1979 ——
The Orchestra gives two concerts to celebrate Sir Adrian Boult's 90th birthday and plays for Sir Robert Mayer's 100th birthday concert. Tour of Austria and West Germany. The Orchestra gives its 1,000th performance at Glyndebourne. Sir Georg Solti succeeds Bernard Haitink as principal conductor.

—— 1980 ——
Eric Bravington retires; Stephen Crabtree becomes managing director. Tour of Japan and Korea.

—— 1981 ——
Helmut Schmidt, Chancellor of West Germany, takes part as a solo pianist in a London Philharmonic recording.

—— 1982 ——
The Orchestra celebrates its golden jubilee.

Foreword

BY HRH THE DUKE OF KENT

As Patron of The London Philharmonic Orchestra I send to all past and present members of the orchestra my warmest congratulations on their Golden Jubilee.

During its half century of existence, the LPO has achieved an enviable reputation as one of the finest orchestras in the world and this says a great deal for the hard work and dedication both of its musicians and of all who work for it.

I look forward to the special year of celebrations which I am sure will be a prelude to another fifty happy and successful years of music-making.

PATRON

Introduction

I cannot remember what was the first symphony orchestra I heard, but I know which was the first whose work I got to know well: the London Philharmonic. This was partly because my Uncle Alex played the violin in it, and could get tickets at a reduced price, but much more because in those days (not long after the war) the LPO was the orchestra that seemed to attract to its podium the largest number of those conducting giants who, even to my youthful musical understanding, were already obviously legends in their own time. The wayward Beecham had by then parted company from the LPO, and opened for business in premises on the Royal side of the street, but the LPO (incidentally, can any musically knowledgeable philologist explain why concert-goers, in speaking of the London orchestras in colloquial terms, abbreviate the LSO to its initials and the Royal Philharmonic to 'the Royal Phil', but always say 'the London Philharmonic'?) had a whole skyful of stars in its eyes. There was the fiery de Sabata, heir to the Toscanini tradition; Furtwängler, that tormented spirit who had stayed behind in Nazi Germany 'to look after German music' and to eat his heart out in sorrow and vain regrets; van Beinum, whose modest, restrained yet intense style seems to have been reborn in Bernard Haitink; and the man who in thirty-six years of concert-going has still never been surpassed for me: Bruno Walter.

A youth just beginning his journey into music *must* have such stars to steer by; he must also have suns and moons, in the form of the composers to whom he gives a similar allegiance. For most young people then (and I should be horrified as well as astonished to learn that it is no longer true) Beethoven was Zeus. Now in those days the Beethoven cycle, in which all the symphonies, and sometimes the concertos too, were played in a series of concerts over a period of a few weeks, was one of the most familiar features of the year's music in London; I heard Walter's cycle, Furtwängler's and van Beinum's, before Klemperer and the brand-new Philharmonia began what became an annual event, and the richness of musical feeling, knowledge and memory the experience provided has lasted the rest of my life. The Beethoven cycle no longer pedals by as regularly as it once did, but I was delighted when Haitink and the LPO revived it at the Festival Hall a few years ago; I went to all the concerts of the series, not only for old time's sake. (In my early music-going days there was no Royal Festival Hall, and many's the LPO Sunday concert I heard from the gods on the stage of the Royal Opera House.)

Flitting from concert-hall to concert-hall, night after night, I suppose I imagined, if I thought of the matter at all, that the orchestral players appeared rather like the *genie* from Aladdin's lamp, with a single rub. I knew nothing in those days of the economics of music, but it does not require long hours with the balance-sheet and the schedule to know that, given the conditions in which the London orchestras have to work, it is a miracle that any music ever gets played at all, let alone that such generally high standards are kept up, year after year.

'Year after year'; and here is the London Philharmonic, my first true love among the orchestras, celebrating its fiftieth anniversary. There can be few conductors, pianists, violinists, cellists of distinction who have never performed with the LPO, but I speak not as a performer but as a member of the audience, and I know I speak for an immense throng when I say that London music (and Sussex music, too, since the LPO became the resident orchestra during the summer at Glyndebourne) has been well served by this still sprightly fifty-year-old. Like all orchestras, it has had its bad times as well as its good, but every year I still scan eagerly the LPO's brochure with its seasons's programmes listed, and it would be a very odd year indeed if I did not immediately circle half a dozen of the concerts as well worth a visit. Any music-lover will agree that the British musical scene would be immeasurably the poorer without the London Philharmonic, and I thank them from my heart for all the hours of music they have given me from those early days to the present. I wish them another half century of happiness, music-making and full houses, and in doing so I wish London audiences another half century of memorable musical evenings.

BERNARD LEVIN
June 1982

THE LONDON PHILHARMONIC ORCHESTRA
LIST OF PLAYERS 1932

First Violins
PAUL BEARD
B. REILLIE
P. FROSTICK
B. H. ANDREWS
L. LEVITUS
E. VIRGO
I. LOSOWSKY
G. WHITAKER
A. AMERY-NICHOLS
D. TAYLOR
N. COMRAS
R. MORLEY
A. BALCH
D. FREEDMAN
A. G. JONES
F. R. DRAKE

Second Violins
GEORGE STRATTON
A. HOPKINSON
H. BALL
W. SPRATT
M. SANDERS
L. STEIN
R. STEEL
A. KIRK
H. COLLINS
C. C. DRAPER
E. MORGAN
W. HULSON
A. FILER
L. G. RICHARDS
E. ROLOFF
H. CHEVREAU

Violas
FRANK HOWARD
J. DYER
W. J. SMITH
J. CLOAD
L. BIRNBAUM
I. SMITH
W. REYNOLDS
G. M. PARKER
B. DAVIS
J. DENMAN
W. FORBES
E. A. CHRISTENSEN

Violoncellos
ANTHONY PINI
J. MOORE
C. L. WILLOUGHBY
J. W. FRANCIS
G. MARINARI
G. ROTH
B. RICKELMAN
T. G. BUDD
F. W. HODGKINSON
D. F. THOMAS

Double-Basses
VICTOR WATSON
J. H. SILVESTER
S. STERLING
H. GREEN
J. HATTON
C. GRAY
P. STANLEY
G. BROOKS
G. HATTON

Flutes
GERALD JACKSON
P. WHITAKER
J. FRANCIS

Piccolo
L. HOPKINSON

Oboes
LÉON GOOSSENS
H. LYONS
W. WHITAKER

Cor Anglais
H. S. GREEN

Clarinets
REGINALD KELL
L. F. COLLINS

E Flat Clarinet
E. J. AUGARDE

Bass Clarinet
A. G. STUTELEY

Bassoons
JOHN ALEXANDRA
G. HOLBROOKE
G. VINTER

Contra-Bassoon
A. ALEXANDRA

Horns
FRANCIS BRADLEY
V. BURROWS
T. WOOD
F. PROBYN

F. HAMILTON
J. PHILLIPS
J. MASON
G. MANNERS
R. WEST

Trumpets
J. H. COZENS
R. DYSON
R. WALTON
H. WILD
F. L. GYP

Trombones
E. GARVIN
F. STEAD
W. H. COLEMAN

Tenor-Tuba
H. SMITH

Tuba
W. SCANNELL

Timpani
J. BRADSHAW

Percussion
M. E. FLYNN
J. HANRAHAN
S. BECKWITH
H. C. WESTON

Harps
MARIE GOOSSENS
MURIEL COLE
JULIA WOLFE

THE LONDON PHILHARMONIC ORCHESTRA
LIST OF PLAYERS 1982

First Violins
DAVID NOLAN *Leader*
RICHARD LAYTON *Sub-Leader*
ROBERT ST. JOHN WRIGHT
ROLAND STANBRIDGE
JOHN KITCHEN
JOHN GREENSMITH
PAUL MANLEY
GEORGE APEL
GEOFFREY LYNN
KENNETH KING
KATHARINE PRICE
MÁIRE DILLON
PHILIP SUTTON
MARILYN GERMAINS
MARIE WILSON, MBE

Second Violins
RUSSELL GILBERT *Principal*
KEITH PASCOE *Co-Principal*
GEOFFREY PRICE
MICHAEL HEALY
KENNETH WESTON
JOHN KUTCHMY
DAVID MARCOU
DAVID MCLAREN
BRIAN PORTER
WOLFGANG KELLERMAN
PETER MAYES
ELEANOR ST. GEORGE
JOHN REID

Violas
RUSEN GÜNES *Principal*
ANTHONY BYRNE *Co-Principal*
JUDY SWAN
MARTIN KOSTER
DAVID GODSELL
ROBERT DUNCAN
WRAYBURN GLASSPOOL
FREDERICK BUXTON
IRMELI RAWSON
ANNE RYCROFT
MAVIS RICHARDS
MICHAEL TURNER

Cellos
ALEXANDER CAMERON *Principal*
MARK JACKSON *Co-Principal*
CATHERINE WILMERS
JOHN LOWDELL
SANTIAGO SABINO CARVALHO
RONALD CALDER
THOMAS FRANCIS
ROGER LUNN
ERNEST GREAVES
JOHN SHARP

Basses
WILLIAM WEBSTER *Principal*
KENNETH GOODE *Co-Principal*
BRYAN SCOTT
LAURENCE LOVELLE

DAVID JAMES
GEORGE NEVISON
GEOFFREY DOWNS
SIMON BENSON

Flutes
MARTIN PARRY *Principal*
CELIA CHAMBERS
ROBIN CHAPMAN

Piccolo
ROBIN CHAPMAN

Oboes
JOAN WHITING
GEOFFREY BROWNE

Cor Anglais
GEOFFREY BROWNE

Clarinets
ROBERT HILL *Principal*
PETER MAUNDER
STEPHEN TRIER

Bass Clarinet
STEPHEN TRIER

Bassoons
JOHN PRICE *Principal*
MICHAEL BOYLE
VALENTINE KENNEDY

Contra Bassoon
VALENTINE KENNEDY

Horns
NICHOLAS BUSCH *Principal*
NIGEL BLACK
PATRICK GARVEY
JOHN ROOKE
IAIN KEDDIE

Trumpets
LAWRENCE EVANS *Principal*
STANLEY WOODS *Co-Principal*
MICHAEL CLOTHIER
SIDNEY ELLISON

Trombones
DEREK JAMES *Principal*
COLIN BUSBY

Bass Trombone
PETER HARVEY

Tuba
PAUL LAWRENCE *Principal*

Timpani
ALAN CUMBERLAND *Principal*

Percussion
KEITH MILLAR *Principal*
NIGEL THOMAS
STEPHEN WARDLE

Harps
JANICE BEVEN *Principal*
DAVID WATKINS

We in Commercial Union Assurance
send warmest congratulations to our friends in the
London Philharmonic Orchestra on their fiftieth anniversary.
Our support for the Orchestra's concerts and tours overseas and in
the United Kingdom has been the basis of many individual
friendships developed over the years and our staff have taken much
pride in this association with one of the world's leading orchestras. It
gave us all particular pleasure when the Commercial Union was
awarded the major prize at the 1981/82 Business Sponsorship of the
Year ceremony, organized by the Association for Business
Sponsorship of the Arts and *The Daily Telegraph*, for the best
corporate programme of sponsorship, and the important part that the
London Philharmonic Orchestra played in the programme was a
major reason for this success. We take additional pride in sponsoring
this anniversary publication in the hope that it will spread the story of
the London Philharmonic Orchestra around the world and help to
bring its special talents to even wider audiences in the future.

The London Philharmonic
Orchestra came into being through
a fit of pique. Sir Thomas Beecham
was a genius on the rostrum, and
also what he himself called a
'musical Maecenas' – a founder of
orchestras. By 1929, when he was
fifty, he had founded more
orchestras than many people hear in
a lifetime. But times were not what
they had been, even for private
fortunes. When the BBC started a
new symphony orchestra, Beecham
hoped for 'closer involvement',
which to him meant total
domination. The BBC, however,
were shy of so flamboyant a
personality, and their orchestra's
direction went elsewhere.

  Sir Thomas's reaction was to put
together a financial consortium to
found the London Philharmonic
Orchestra. Two of the new
directors left almost as soon as they
were appointed, and two remained:
Samuel Courtauld and Robert
Mayer.

For the leading players in his new London Philharmonic, Beecham shamelessly raided both the new BBC Symphony Orchestra and the London Symphony, tempting away celebrated virtuosi with high fees. For the rest he filled the ranks with young players whom he could shape to his will.

The new Orchestra's first concert, promoted by the Royal Philharmonic Society, was preceded by twelve rehearsals. The concert took place on 7 October 1932. The veteran critic Ernest Newman wrote in *The Sunday Times*:

Sir Thomas Beecham's new orchestra . . . began its operations in Queen's Hall on Friday evening. . . . He began with a performance of Berlioz's Carnaval Romain *overture that had an air about it of 'You Londoners want to know what an orchestra ought to be like? Well, just listen to this.' The demonstration was certainly complete enough; nothing so electrifying has been heard in a London concert room for years. The tone was magnificent, the precision perfect, the reading a miracle of fire and beauty, and the enthusiasm of the audience could not have been greater. . . .* [1]

Beecham and the new Orchestra rehearsing at Liverpool on their first tour, March 1933.

At one of the earliest London Philharmonic Sunday Concerts in November 1932, the sixteen-year-old Yehudi Menuhin played a programme of violin concertos: the Bach and Mozart were conducted by Sir Thomas, while the Elgar concerto was directed by the seventy-five-year-old composer himself.

The name 'London Philharmonic' suggested that the new Orchestra would take on the long-established Royal Philharmonic Society concerts, and so they did. Beecham also arranged other engagements. These included the Robert Mayer Concerts for Children, the Royal Choral Society concerts, and the Courtauld-Sargent Concert Club, which brought in Malcolm Sargent as conductor of many concerts. There were numerous gramophone recordings. Last but not least, there was the International Season of opera at Covent Garden (of which Beecham himself was artistic director) and the Russian Ballet.

By 1935 LPO players enjoyed a guaranteed income. Thomas Russell, a violist who joined the Orchestra that year, recalled:

It was not unusual for us to do no concerts for a fortnight, and still go to the office at the end of each week to collect our salaries. It was also not unusual for the payment of our salaries to be seriously delayed, and I remember one occasion . . . when the players became very restive at a prolonged delay. The conductor on that day, Dr Sargent, spent some time in contacting people from whom money was due to the Orchestra, and thus made it possible for us to be paid. Dr Sargent was the most popular man in the profession at that moment! [2]

COURTAULD SARGENT CONCERTS

QUEEN'S HALL

...RAMME R...

...AY 10th

CORAL SOCIETY
ALBERT HALL, W.

H.M. THE KING

4th February, 1933 at 2.30 p.m.

...n Egypt - Handel

Miss ISOBEL B...
Miss NOËL E...
Miss MARIE ...
Mr. FRANK ...
Mr. FRANK...
Mr. FRANK...

LO...
PHILHARMON...

Dr. MALCO...

Prices: Stalls, 8/6; Arena, 6...
Gallery...

obtainable from Box Office...

The Royal Philharmonic Society
INSTITUTED 1813
Patrons—THEIR MAJESTIES THE KING AND QUEEN
For particulars of membership, apply to the Hon. Secretary, Royal Philharmonic Society, 19 Berners Street, W.
One Hundred and Twenty-first Season, 1932-33.

QUEEN'S HALL
8.15 p.m.
Sole Lessees MESSRS. CHAPPELL & Co., LTD.

...AINING FIVE CONCERTS

Stenka Razine
...Pianoforte Concerto (First performance)   Glazounov
...heherazade   Szymanovsky
...Conductor: NICOLAI MALKO   Solo Pianoforte: JAN SMETERLIN
                                                     Rimsky-Korsakov

BRAHMS CENTENARY CONCERT
...ations on the St. Anthony Chorale of Haydn
...le Concerto for Violin and Violoncello   Brahms
...iolin: JELLY D'ARANYI   Solo Violoncello: GASPAR CASSADO
         Conductor: SIR THOMAS BEECHAM

...: "Les deux Aveugles de Toledé"   Mehul
...Faëry Hills   Bax
...y No. 8, in F major   Beethoven
...e Fantastique   Berlioz
         Conductor: SIR THOMAS BEECHAM

...William Tell"   Rossini
...ertante, for Violin, Viola and Orchestra   Mozart
...hony (First performance)   Sibelius
...2, in C
...LBERT SAMMONS.   Solo Viola: LIONEL TERTIS
         Conductor: SIR THOMAS BEECHAM   Tchaikovsky

...in G major   Handel
...First performance in England)   Pizzetti
         (Conducted by THE COMPOSER)
...C major
...nductor: SIR THOMAS BEECHAM   Schubert
...HILHARMONIC ORCHESTRA

...hilharmonic."
...has been heard in a London Concert Room for years."

...2/- unreserved (inclusive Tax). Obtainable at the
...& Co., Ltd., 159, New Bond Street, London...
...and all Libraries.

CENTRAL HALL, WESTMINSTER, S.W.1

ROBERT MAYER CONCERTS FOR CHILDREN

1932
October 22nd
November 12th
December 3rd

Jan. 7th & 28th
February 18th
March 11th

1933

TENTH SEASON, 1932-33

Fifth Concert—Saturday Morning, January 28th
At ELEVEN a.m. sharp
Doors will be opened at 10-40 and will be closed during performance.

PROGRAMME

Sinfonia Church Cantata No. 98 ... ...   Bach
Concerto for Piano and Orchestra in B major (K.V. 595) Mozart
      Allegro, Larghetto, Allegro.
      Soloist: ARTUR SCHNABEL
Overture: "Freischütz" ...   Weber

MALCOLM SARGENT

In the autumn of 1936, a London Philharmonic tour of Germany was organized under the aegis of the German Government. Many of the Orchestra had doubts about sponsorship by the Nazis, including Thomas Russell. But as he wrote:

It is doubtful whether Sir Thomas even considered this aspect of the matter. Wrapped up as he was in the cares and details of an artistic life, scornful of most forms of orthodox government, and ready to scoff at official cultural pretensions, he merely recognized that the tour would add lustre to the reputation of his Orchestra. [3]

Hitler and other members of the Nazi Government attended the opening concert of the tour on 13 November in Berlin. Russell recalled:

It was very much a State occasion, and I was extremely amused as we sat on the platform waiting for the audience to settle down, to watch the antics of the fervent Nazis who greeted all those they knew with the fascist salute. . . . [4]

After the concert, members of the Orchestra celebrated with their colleagues in the Berlin Philharmonic. Thomas Russell remembered:

. . . Sir Thomas, who appeared to have enjoyed the dinner after his successful concert, stayed behind, and when we began to move away from the tables, he climbed on to one of them and, to the delighted surprise of the Berliners, conducted two choruses of The More We Are Together. *. . . Soon after this display of unconventionality I looked for Sir Thomas, but he had left unobserved, having discovered with faultless timing when the party had reached the point when his assistance was no longer required. Our conviviality went on well into the night until, with the introduction of Schnapps between the beers, many of those present had ceased to acknowledge everyday ideas and conventions.* [5]

Gradually the Nazi web tightened over Europe. Among the refugees to arrive in England was Dr Berta Geissmar, who had been Wilhelm Furtwängler's secretary in Berlin. She became Beecham's secretary. In May 1937 she joined both conductors at the head table when the LPO gave a dinner at the Savoy to entertain the visiting Berlin Philharmonic. To the assembled company Beecham observed:

While we were in Germany I made thirty-nine speeches, the same number as the articles of the English Church, and every one of them was different. In reply to my orations, a high German official of one designation or another made a similar number of speeches, each of which was identical, thus showing the superiority of the Teutonic mind. [6]

Beecham conducting the LPO in the pit at Covent Garden.

As the forces of war gathered, the London Philharmonic was to share one of the last State Concerts with the Vic-Wells Ballet. Early in 1939 the preparations were watched by Berta Geissmar:

While the Continent was a prey to political convulsions, the Royal Opera House was the scene of a friendly demonstration of the first order. On the occasion of the State visit of the French President and Mme Lebrun to England, a command performance took place.

ROYAL OPERA

COVENT GARDEN

·MCMXXXIX·

Mar. 22nd

The old and dignified Opera House was decorated for the occasion with the finest tapestries and French furniture to be found in England. A fragment of tapestry had been found woven in honour of the marriage of Charles I and Henrietta Maria of France in 1625, and it bore the following words, so significant also for the present occasion: 'Aimez vous, les Uns les Autres.'

This tapestry was hung at the entrance of the Royal anteroom and greeted the arriving guest of honour. The Court, the Corps Diplomatique, *members of English society, and many high dignitaries were assembled. . . .*[7]

With the outbreak of the Second
World War in the summer of 1939
came a crisis for the Orchestra.
Thomas Russell wrote:

*The costs of maintaining such a
body of musicians were rapidly
outstripping the means of even the
wealthiest, and one by one they
retired. . . . In 1939, just as the war
broke out, Sir Thomas announced that
he could not keep the Orchestra in
being. He conducted the liquidation
meeting with a skill similar to that
which he had so often displayed at
concerts. . . .*

*Such a defeat to a conductor with a
pocketful of contracts to appear with
orchestras in other parts of the world was
one thing. For members of the Orchestra,
with no such attractive future before
them, it spelt disaster.*

*A few of the older players schemed to keep
the Orchestra alive. With no knowledge of
concert-giving beyond playing their parts in
the orchestra, they discussed Company Law
over a pint of beer, studied railway timetables
over lunch, and, as soon as they had acquired
an office, a typewriter and some headed
notepaper, learnt the science of concert
promotion the hard way.*[8]

Charles Gregory, principal horn
and chairman (standing) meeting
with other members in the early
days of the independent
Orchestra. Thomas Russell wrote:

*They began by entirely reforming
their own organization, turning
it into a co-operative body,
controlled only by players elected
for three years' service.
Although these chosen players
accepted many responsibilities,
they received nothing extra for
their pains except the lively
criticism of their colleagues. . . .*

*We stood at the end of an
epoch, and mixed our regrets
with hope. . . .*[9]

They called the new company
'Musical Culture Ltd'.

Thomas Russell was chosen as secretary, despite his well-known sympathies with the political left, because he was one of the most articulate members of the Orchestra.

One of his first actions was to commission a monogram for the Orchestra from Sir Edwin Lutyens. Another was to found an official magazine: the editing, much of the writing, and all of the planning for the bi-monthly issues fell upon Russell himself.

LONDON *Philharmonic Post*

e Reasons Behind the Philharmonic Post

ue of this Bulletin marks a new step in British music. No such link between an orchestra
public has, to our knowledge, ever been published ; its possibilities are legion. If this
ress on the Appeal it is because we have been so overwhelmed by the
we could think of little else. Subsequent issues will contain

Britain is an

Up to the time of his departure, Beecham continued to conduct the Orchestra, and in January 1940 launched an appeal. £2000 resulted, enough to keep the Orchestra in being for a further few months.

April 1940: Sir Thomas Beecham, preparing to live in Australia and the New World for several years, was given a 'bon voyage' upper by the Orchestra. He was flanked by the new chairman, Charles Gregory (right) and the secretary, Thomas Russell. Russell ecalled:

. . Gregory gave a sincere and sensitive speech in which he conveyed our understanding of the profound loss we were about to uffer. The greatest tribute that could be paid to Beecham was that, in spite of all his vagaries from which the orchestral usician had suffered from time to time, he had only to conduct a successful concert to convince them all that only music attered. [10]

By the summer of 1940, as the first air raids over London began, there was no money left. In desperation Russell turned to J. B. Priestley, asking him to make a personal appeal at a special concert.

QUEEN'S HALL - LANGHAM PLACE

(Sole Lessees - Messrs. Chappell & Co., Ltd.)

Thursday, July 18th, 1940, at 8.15 p.m.

MUSICAL CULTURE LIMITED

presents

A

MUSICAL MANIFESTO

Speaker :

J. B. PRIESTLEY

THE LONDON PHILHARMONIC ORCHESTRA

Conductors :

SIR ADRIAN BOULT
BASIL CAMERON
DR. MALCOLM SARGENT

Solo Pianoforte :

EILEEN JOYCE

Programme and
Notes price 6d.

Russell described the concert:

On the night every seat was sold – a rare event at that period. . . . Although many of us were unaware of the desperate position of the nation, the dangers and disasters of Dunkirk turned the national mind to a serious mood. It was to this mood that Priestley's warm, reasoned humanity made its appeal. . . .

The next few days were postal chaos. . . . I am convinced that there was something underneath the response far greater than the direct desire to help a symphony orchestra. . . . The LPO became a symbol of reality, and attracted support from all those who saw and hoped beyond the present.[11]

One of the best results of the 'Musical Manifesto' was a proposal from Jack Hylton, who controlled many theatres up and down the country. Russell wrote:

His idea was to present the LPO on a music-hall or theatre tour in various large industrial centres. . . . He wanted us to give a normal programme and to trust to the good sense and taste of the ordinary man-in-the-street to make the thing a success.

Hylton was not intending to leave the success of the venture to chance. He organized a huge publicity campaign with all the resources at his disposal. . . . This publicity did a great deal in making the people outside the normal concert-going audiences aware that they possessed a cultural instrument of which they could be proud. It gave us an approach to the people of the whole country on which we were able to build a solid foundation.[12]

For every hour of successful music-making, the Orchestra spent many hours in hazardous wartime travel and many a cold night on railway platforms in towns where hotels were full or closed.

Through the Hylton tours the Orchestra regularly gave two and even three concerts a day.

PALACE THEATRE MANCHESTER

MONDAY NEXT FOR ONE WEEK 3-30 and 5-45

JACK HYLTON PRESENTS THE LONDON PHILHARMONIC ORCHESTRA

Conductors—Dr. MALCOLM SARGENT, BASIL CAMERON, ERIC COATES
Leader—THOMAS MATTHEWS.
Solo Pianist—EILEEN JOYCE

MONDAY

1st PERFORMANCE
Beethoven Programme.
Egmont, Minuet in G. Fifth Symphony, Leonora III., and Ballet Music "Rosamunde" (Schubert).
Conductor : Dr. MALCOLM SARGENT.

2nd PERFORMANCE
"Merry Wives of Windsor," Air on G String (Bach), Scheherazade, Midsummer Night's Dream Suite, La Calinda (Delius), Carnaval Romain (Berlioz).
Conductor : Dr. MALCOLM SARGENT.

TUESDAY

1st PERFORMANCE
ONE HOUR OF ERIC COATES' WORKS :
Overture "Merrymakers," Suite "Summerdays," Three Bears, Symphonic Rhapsody "I Pitched My Lonely Caravan," Bird Songs at Eventide, Scène de Bal, Suite "Three Men," Knightsbridge March.
Conductor : ERIC COATES.
Lohengrin Prelude, Valse Triste, Carmen Suite.
Conductor : Dr. MALCOLM SARGENT.

2nd PERFORMANCE
ONE HOUR OF ERIC COATES' WORKS :
Overture "Merrymakers," Suite "Summerdays," Three Bears, Symphonic Rhapsody "I Pitched My Lonely Caravan," Bird Songs at Eventide, Scène de Bal, Suite "Three Men," Knightsbridge March.
Conductor : ERIC COATES.
Lohengrin Prelude, Valse Triste, Carmen Suite.
Conductor : Dr. MALCOLM SARGENT.

WEDNESDAY

1st PERFORMANCE
Barber of Seville, Symphony in G Minor (Mozart), Capriccio Espagnole, Finlandia, Irmelin (Delius), Prince Igor Dances.
Conductor : Dr. MALCOLM SARGENT.

2nd PERFORMANCE
Zampa, Caprice Viennois, Pathetic Symphony (Tschaikovsky), Water Music (Handel), Hungarian March (Berlioz).
Conductor : Dr. MALCOLM SARGENT.

THURSDAY

1st PERFORMANCE
Trojan March (Berlioz), Fifth Symphony (Schubert), Nutcracker Suite, La Boutique Fantasque, Meistersinger Overture.
Conductor : Dr. MALCOLM SARGENT.

2nd PERFORMANCE
Vienna Woods, Hebrides, Symphony No. VII, in A (Beethoven), Lyric Suite (Grieg), "1812."
Conductor : Dr. MALCOLM SARGENT.

FRIDAY

1st PERFORMANCE
Overture "Mignon" (Thomas), In the Steppes of Central Asia (Borodin), Symphony No. IV. (Dvorák), Lyric Suite (Grieg), Andante from Cassation in G (Mozart), Capriccio Italien (Tschaikovsky).
Conductor : BASIL CAMERON.

2nd PERFORMANCE
Russlan and Ludmilla (Glinka), Two Songs Without Words (Mendelssohn), Dance of the Hours, Overture "William Tell," Hungarian Rhapsody No. II, Rhapsody in Blue, On Hearing the First Cuckoo, Blue Danube Waltz, Finlandia.
Conductor : BASIL CAMERON.

SATURDAY

1st PERFORMANCE
March Tannhäuser (Act II), Dance of the Hours, Andante Cantabile, Overture "William Tell," Hungarian Rhapsody No. II, Rhapsody in Blue, On Hearing the First Cuckoo, Two Hungarian Dances, Overture "Die Fledermaus."
Conductor : BASIL CAMERON.

2nd PERFORMANCE
Overture "Light Cavalry," In the Steppes of Central Asia (Borodin), Lyric Suite (Grieg), Capriccio Italien (Tschaikovsky), Valse "Sleeping Beauty" (Tschaikovsky), Ave Maria (Schubert), Ballet Music "Le Cid" (Massenet), Overture "Masaniello" (Auber).
Conductor : BASIL CAMERON.

Box Office Open 10—8. RETAIN FOR REFERENCE 'Phone : CENtral 0184.

POPULAR SYMPHONY CONCERTS

Under the auspices of MUSICAL CULTURE LTD.

JACK HYLTON presents the

LONDON PHILHARMONIC ORCHESTRA

Leader - THOMAS MATTHEWS

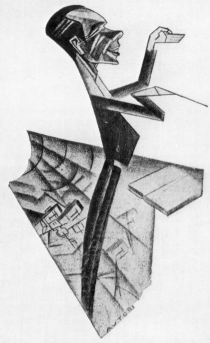

Conductor : Dr. MALCOLM SARGENT

Against this background, no choice of conductor could have been more happy than Malcolm Sargent. With his svelte figure, his incisive manner and his conscious showmanship, added to the enthusiasm which he so easily displayed and aroused, he made the audiences feel at once that they were in for a good time. At many of the earlier performances, he adapted his method of speaking to children to an adult audience, and this created a favourable atmosphere for the music which followed. [13]

The LPO was giving concerts in places where no symphony orchestra had ever been seen. Among the greatest successes of the wartime tours were concerts conducted by the great Viennese tenor, Richard Tauber.

Tour visits required careful preparation.

Monday, July 21st. Pal___ Miners Institute___
Edwards, Secretary ___rs Institute. He is___
hard work, and will ___nly have to be "loc___
certain amount of c___ ___n. Whole day should___
£100 for afternoon, ___ng total of £262. If he is present, Lord Howard de Walden
should be seen and ___hanked etc: for his patronage!

Tuesday, July 22nd. ___ Manager of Pier Pavilion Coy: ___ ___urner Pilling.
Agreement: We to rec___ ___ of the ticket sales, and full pro___ ___ights, apart fro___
a 2d. in the shillin___ ___ion for sellers. Gross capacity figu___ ___x: £384.

Wednesday, July 23rd. ___ ___ments Mar___ ___ C. Priestley E___ ___greement:
We to receive 75% of t___ ___, and f___ ___ rights, apart ___ ___ in the
shilling commission for ___ ___ross ___ £250.

Thursday, July 24th. Loc___ ___, 3 Clough Str___ ___ ___el:
2782.) Special arrangement ___ ___s ca___ ___ ___ng
200 standing.

Friday, July 25th. Mr. B.W. ___ ___s. He is a master
at Grammar School, and has bee___ ___ents. Actual booking
are in hands of Miss Burton, M___ ___ork House, Doncaster.
Monetary arrangement for after___ ___ld, and another 6d per
child to be added by Director ___ ___ a limited number of
public seats at one of the mat___ ___rethewey (a friend of Mr.
Appleby's) who is, I understa___ ___ike that of the Schools
Musical Association in Donca___

PALACE (MINERS INSTITUTE) RHOS

MONDAY, JULY 21st, at 3 and 7-30.
Under the patronage of LORD HOWARD de WALDEN.

MUSICAL CULTURE Ltd. presents
FOR THE FIRST TIME IN HISTORY!
Special Visit of the Entire

LONDON PHILHARMONIC ORCHESTRA

(FULL STRENGTH — 70 MASTER PLAYERS)

Conducted by

RICHARD TAUBER

In Two Popular Programmes, including :
Aft.: SCHUBERT'S 5th Symphony : Freischutz Overture (*Weber*)
L'Arlesienne Suite (*Bizet*).
Even.: BEETHOVEN'S "PASTORAL" SYMPHONY ;
Oberon Overture (*Weber*) ; Tales from the Vienna Woods (*Strauss*).

ALL SEATS BOOKABLE IN ADVANCE NOW
Aft. 5/-, 3/- & 2/- (500 seats reserved for school-
Even. 5/-, 4/- 3/- & 2/-   children at 1/-)
at PALACE BOX OFFICE (Rhos 53)
                                  open daily 11—1, 3—9
also through CRANE & SONS, 40 Regent Street,
                WREXHAM (Tel. 2563).
All postal applications (accompanied by stamped envelope) and
special enquires to: Councillor J. T. Edwards, J.P., Miners
                Institute, RHOS (Tel. 53).

Musical Culture Ltd., 295, Regent Street, London, W.1.

Parnells The Printers, Ltd.

Beecham's former secretary, Berta Geissmar, had remained in London with the Orchestra. She wrote:

In the beginning of 1941 . . . there was a need to feed air raid wardens, rescue squads, firemen, demolition workers, and the bombed people themselves. . . . Friends of the London Philharmonic Orchestra had the idea of providing a mobile canteen, bearing the name of the Orchestra. . . . On weekdays it was on duty for defence workers, on Saturday afternoons and Sundays it was in action in front of Queen's Hall, decorated with posters advertising the concerts of the London Philharmonic Orchestra. . . .

Crowds gathered in the interval round the canteen, where popular Covent Garden singers were to be seen distributing tea or washing up the cups.[14]

After a concert on Saturday afternoon, 10 May 1941, the Orchestra left their instruments in Queen's Hall ready for rehearsal the next day. That night hundreds of German bombers raided London, and the following morning the players arrived to find Queen's Hall a smoking ruin and their instruments destroyed.

For Sir Henry Wood, who had already conducted the Orchestra several times, it seemed at that moment the end of a life's work.

Thomas Russell recalled:

The rehearsal which was to have taken place . . . was cancelled so that those who had lost their instruments could beg, borrow or steal replacements for the afternoon's concert. Those who had instruments to spare went home to collect them for the benefit of less fortunate colleagues.

The only alteration which we allowed in our plans was to delay the starting time for half an hour to give those members of the public who had been unaware of the disaster time to go from

Langham Place to [the Duke's Hall of the Royal Academy of Music in] Marylebone Road. Mr Taylor and Mr Matthews of the Queen's Hall management . . . took charge of the ticket situation, selling tickets and redirecting the public from a table on the pavement outside the ruins.[15]

G QUEEN'S HALL LANGHAM PLACE, W.1.
Sole Lessees Messrs. Chappell & Co., Ltd.,
Sunday Afternoon, MAY 11th, at 2.30
SECOND L.P.O. SUMMER
SUNDAY CONCERT
LONDON PHILHARMONIC ORCHESTRA
STALL (Reserved)
Row 14 No. 36 5/-
COMPLIMENTARY
Entrance and Exit in Langham Place, Door No. 4
MUSICAL CULTURE, Ltd., 295, Regent Street, W.1.

QUEEN'S
Sunday, 11th
at 2.30
SECOND
L.P.O. SUMMER
SUNDAY CONCERT
London Philharmonic
Orchestra
STALL
Reserved - 5/-
Row 14 No. 36

Once again Russell and his committee took quick action:

As soon as the question of security allowed, an appeal for instruments was made over the wireless, and the response proved in a new way the affection which the Orchestra had already won. . . . [16]

OPEN LETTER TO ALL WHO HAVE OFFERED INSTRUMENTS TO THE LONDON PHILHARMONIC ORCHESTRA.

FRIENDS,

In response to our appeal after the destruction of Queen's Hall, there were innumerable calls at this office, countless offers by telephone, and scores of gifts arrived by parcel post and carrier. In addition we received some 3,000 letters offering instruments on loan, for sale, or as gifts.

The utmost kindness characterised these letters, and the Committee of the Orchestra wished to answer them promptly and personally, but this was impossible, and a duplicated form was sent in reply.

The Committee is deeply grateful for these letters: appreciates their friendliness, and would like to return thanks to the many correspondents who offered instruments. Some letters from the very aged and young folks have been answered individually, but many others, even though the Orchestra was in London it generally had ... thing could be done.

The loss of Queen's Hall left the Orchestra without a base. Russell took the lease of the Orpheum Theatre, Golders Green:

We commandeered the building, which was entirely unstaffed, and proceeded to run it in our own way. As only two or three of us were available at the time, every duty devolved on us. . . . Between stopping leaks in the roof to stoking the boilers (when we had first secured a coal supply) there were a thousand and one jobs to which we had to adapt ourselves. [16]

But for a time the Orchestra once more had a home.

Philharmonic

By **THOMAS RUSSELL**

Introduction by **J. B. PRIESTLEY**

This book, now in the press, is written by the Editor of the *Philharmonic Post*, organiser of the work of the London Philharmonic Orchestra since 1939, and a playing member of the Orchestra since 1935. The author deals with many aspects of the symphony orchestra: its growth, its leaders, its conductors, its finance, halls and programmes, its audiences and its future. The illustrations are by Alan Gregory.

Mr. PRIESTLEY *says* :

" . . . *clearly the product of a lively and courageous intelligence. His book is a contribution to our musical life, and I am sure that a host of readers will soon agree with me, and will be thankful that by some private miracle, during his busy days and nights with his orchestra, he has found time to produce these stimulating chapters.*"

HUTCHINSON
Price **7**s. **6**d.

How many cold nights have I frozen in the box office, selling tickets to the thin trickle of public who braved the weather to secure seats for the following Sunday's concert. . . . On Sunday, the trickle grew to a flood although we had to wait and shiver all day for it. . . . By the time the last person had gone into the hall, or when the last disappointed person had gone away disconsolate, we were too tired and dazed even to listen to the music.[17]

But Russell was indefatigable. Looking towards the Orchestra's tenth anniversary in 1942, he found time to write a book on the entire theory and practice of running a symphony orchestra. Entitled *Philharmonic*, it was first published by Hutchinson and later by Penguin.

Every chance was taken, each opportunity explored to further the Orchestra's precarious fortunes. An Arts Club was started by John Amis to bring distinguished speakers. The artist Edmond Kapp was commissioned to make a series of drawings to record the Orchestra in action at a critical moment in its history. In the drawing below, the principal trumpet is Malcolm Arnold.

Kapp '43

L.P.O. under Braithwaite in an Airplane-Factory. 4000 War-workers listen to Haydn and Grieg during lunch in the Canteen

ROYAL ALBERT HALL

Manager - C. S. Taylor

DUNKIRK ANNIVERSARY CONCERT

PRESENTED BY BARONESS RAVENSDALE
FOR THE CHILDREN OF GREAT BRITAIN
SPONSORED BY THE *NEWS CHRONICLE*

THURS. JUNE 3, 1943, at 7 p.m.

MYRA HESS
IRENE SCHARRER
ALEXANDRA CHOIR

Conductor - Charles Proctor

LONDON PHILHARMONIC
ORCHESTRA   Leader - Jean Pougnet

SIR ADRIAN BOULT

(By permission of the B.B.C.)

TRUMPETERS
FROM THE
ROYAL MILITARY SCHOOL OF MUSIC
Conducted by BANDMASTER NALDEN, Mus. Bac.
By permission of the Commandant - Major A. T. B. Bignold-de Cologan, T.D.

ORGANIST - - ARNOLD GREIR

TICKETS :
21/-, 15/-, 12/6, 10/6, 7/6, 5/-, 3/6 & 2/6
Boxes : Grand Tier (10 seats) and Loggia (8 seats)
21/- per seat.   Second tier (5 seats) 10/6 per seat
FROM ALBERT HALL, S.W.7 (KEN 3661) and Agencies.

OVER

During the summer of 1942 the Orchestra first appeared at the Proms (now transferred from Queen's Hall to the Royal Albert Hall) under Sir Henry Wood.

Other appearances in London were relatively few as the war ground slowly on.

The grandest of all documents and all advertisements would be a full-length film about the London Philharmonic Orchestra and its history. The Government had intended to fund *Battle for Music* for propaganda use; at the eleventh hour it decided to pull out. But private funds were found and production began in 1943. Thomas Russell recalled the filming:

Members of the first committee and a few of the players were given parts approximating to those which they had played in real life. . . .

Thus it came about that our first appearance in front of the camera was as actors and not as musicians. And it began as a terrifying experience. Whether the powerful lights, or the repetition of phrases dulled our minds, or whether the camera itself was the culprit it is difficult to say, but no sooner did the moment for sound-recording arrive than every word departed beyond reach. . . . Yards of film were wasted on my inability to utter the simplest phrases.[18]

This is the true story of one of the world's greatest o The struggle of eighty men, against every misfortune tha bring, to preserve for us one of our greatest possess London Philharmonic Orchestra.

Truth is said to be stranger than fiction. In this p truth—acted by the men themselves—tells of triun disaster bravely faced with unquenchable humour a shows the inner workings of a great business whose not to make profits, but to give joy and beauty to a wor to preserve those very things. For this is a love story, an its pages walk figures such as J. B. Priestley, Dr. Malcolr Sir Adrian Boult, Jack Hylton—maestro of jazz, and fingered Moiseiwitsch. . . .

In the years that preceded the war, the L.P.O. as th Philharmonic Orchestra is universally known, built itself world famous conductors to the perfection that made its byword amongst music lovers. But many of these people hear the orchestra on records, or on the radio, and se infrequent intervals. It is at Covent Garden Opera Hou was to be the last performance of " Tristan & Isolde, picture opens. No one believed war was imminent. glittering crowd, the tiaras, the jewels, the ermine. The as the last notes die away and the curtain falls.

Then the orchestra. Talk of holidays. The ballet th start afterwards . . . and then over beaches and seasi over a country at play came the news of war. But w news that London was being evacuated. And sudden y —eighty men trained for years—found themselves fac ruptcy—the backers had left, music was finished.

Even then, amidst this chaos and disaster, the men f this could be an opportunity—the one they had hop come in a very different form—the chance to give their to a select few, but to all people in every walk of life. Th of the company wished to wind it up. You have no mo theatres are shut. Give up, get jobs—be sensible.

But headed by Tom Russell, viola, Gregory and Bradle horn players, Morley, 1st violin, and Stead of the tron committee faced creditors and company solicitors. For own company and looked for work. Share and share the rule. But during the weary weeks of rehearsal to spirits up there was nothing to share, except the convi when the sudden shock of war subsided, the nation w music and the arts and entertainment as much as muniti

It wasn't easy all this. Wives and sweethearts don't

Thomas Russell, Francis Bradley and Charles Gregory re-enacting the scene in the autumn of 1939 when they told the Orchestra that they had borrowed enough money for the players' rail fares t Cardiff, where they could take up their first engagement as an independent body.

men in such straits. Musicians must eat, and only by
 and helping each other were they tided over till the first
 a Cardiff cinema was obtained.
tant Lambert conducted " Romeo and Juliet," and only a
rdrafts and pawntickets told of how they managed to get
 Their reception was terrific and the rest of the short tour
rmous success in everything but money. The houses were
fares and food left little over. Bedrooms were an unknown
to these men of the Royal Opera House.
 Russell's idea to link up with the French in a series of
French concerts. His trip to Paris. His escape just ahead
Germans. His miserable return to the orchestra rehearsing
Warwick Braithwaite, waiting and hoping.
 a miracle happened. A call from Jack Hylton—now
ario, theatre owner. Jack would take a chance. Their
nfected him. He would back them in a tour of provincial
halls.
spell had broken. With Dr. Malcolm Sargent, Warwick
vaite and Constant Lambert conducting. With Eileen
and Moiseiwitsch at the piano, they toured the country.
raid, death and destruction, they played and through the
s the people came.
at this peak, the air raids became deadly. The theatres
 Money again short. It was now that J. B. Priestley came
r aid. Alone, he arranged what he insisted on calling a
l Manifesto at the Queens Hall. The people that he wished
act came under the joint stimulus of his and the L.P.O.'s
 . . the same people who had left them to their fate in those
ays of war. But J.B. in his own inimitable manner, took
eques from them, Sir Adrian Boult and others conducted
 day was saved.
 had ideas of taking a theatre of their own—a home of
 Tom found one, the Orpheum at Golders Green. The
 agreed to a convenient lease. At last they could put into
 all they preached.
ng that night's blitz, the Queens Hall burned to the ground.
 all their instruments were lost in the fire. This was the
st blow.
this time fate stepped in to help them. The B.B.C. broad-
eir misfortune and from homes of rich and poor, from
ounty town and hamlet in the country, came the response.
amusing relics, some pathetic, but the orchestra was re-
ed, the theatre re-taken and the people came and that tumul-
eception repaid all they suffered in their battle for music. . .

The script rarely reached its final form until a few minutes before the summary rehearsal, so that this had to be learned in a hurry. . . . The scenes in which a few of us from the Orchestra were starred were, of course, not acted in the ordinary sense of the word. But in spite of this they gave an impression of sincerity to which our naïve efforts added a truer quality.[19]

hn Kuchmy (left,
oking at his Amati
olin):
*We were fools to try to
arry on in wartime.'*

*Maurice Ward (viola):
And yet, how long does
 take to build up such
n orchestra as ours?
Ve couldn't let that
isappear.'*

The list of stars included Sir Adrian Boult, Dr Sargent, Constant Lambert and Warwick Braithwaite, with Eileen Joyce (who had gone with us on the first Hylton tours) and Moiseiwitsch. J. B. Priestley and Jack Hylton appeared in the scenes of their fortunate interventions, and the film added glamour to its human interest. . . . [20]

Using a popular cinema technique of the period, one sequence showed Benno Moiseiwitsch with the London Philharmonic Orchestra under Constant Lambert superimposed on the rushing wheels of an express train to illustrate how the players sped from city to city throughout the war.

present

TTLE for MUSIC

Produced & Directed by DONALD TAYLOR

Y OF THE LONDON PHILHARMONIC ORCHESTRA

J. B. PRIESTLEY

THOMAS RUSSELL   JACK HYLTON

RAITHWAITE   CONSTANT LAMBERT   SIR ADRIAN BOULT   Dr. MALCOLM SARGENT

ANGLO-AMERICAN
FILM CORPORATION, LTD.

PORATION LTD.
phone:- GERRARD 3202-9

BRITISH NATIONAL FILMS, LTD
NATIONAL STUDIOS ELSTREE

A London Philharmonic performance of Beethoven's Fifth Symphony interrupted by an air raid threat: a scene from the film in which Malcolm Sargent tells the audience that, as Beethoven's music cannot be destroyed by Hitler, the Orchestra intends to carry on to the end of the performance.

In 1944 Russell persuaded his committee to purchase the long lease of an entire house in Welbeck Street for £9000. With flying bombs coming into operation, it was a considerable risk. But from that day the Orchestra has enjoyed fine office space in central London.

Russell's young colleague George Barker wrote an article about the office and its staff for the *Philharmonic Post* (revived after a hiatus caused by eighteen months' paper shortage). A drawing of the staff by Alan Gregory shows Russell supporting the poster on the right, the Orchestra's concerts manager Adolph Borsdorf on the telephone and Barker himself at the top right.

A SLIM London house in Welbeck Street. Behind its stream-lined facade lie the classical proportions of eighteenth century London. Such a house is 53. On its lintel might be inscribed the words :—

> " O brave new world
> That hath such creatures in it."

But the manners of an elegant age have passed with the old fanlight and the wrought-iron balcony. No longer does the Concert Director arrive in a brougham or the Publicity Manager upon a horse. In their places are harassed administrators making up on foot the time lost in unpunctual trains. Yet it is pleasant and sentimental to reflect that a 53, much the same in general shape and appearance, must have been there when Mozart and Haydn came to London and many a time Handel, with his head full of Italian operas, may have passed it by.

On a plate by the door is inscribed the legend—" London Philharmonic Orchestra, Limited," followed by " Musical Culture, Limited," and " L.P.P., Ltd.", and underneath the name of the tenant of the top floor, " Mutual Broadcasting." And that is all the outward sign of the changes which time has wrought in concert promotion since the age of Mozart and the sedan chair.

The administration of a great orchestra demands certain specified services, some of them obvious, others less so. Among the obvious ones are publicity, concert direction and accountancy, orchestral management and librarian. Among the less obvious are the educational and public relation services. These all have their residence at 53, Welbeck Street, and from an internal point of view a nice balance has to be preserved between that section of the staff whose primary qualifications are musical and those whose primary qualifications are efficiency in business routine. The unfortunate gentleman whose greying hair testifies to the delicacy with which this situation has to be handled is the general manager, and he deserves first place in the sympathy and consideration of followers of the orchestra. All purchasers of Philharmonic programmes should note with added interest the name of Leigh Bilderbeck Frost at the foot of the page containing the names of the players, for it is he who acts as the buffer state between nations who, though not in any sense at war, nevertheless eye each other at times with a certain degree of alarm and suspicion. That he is successful speaks volumes for the wisdom of the orchestra in employing a man who can combine objectivity and warm human sympathy.

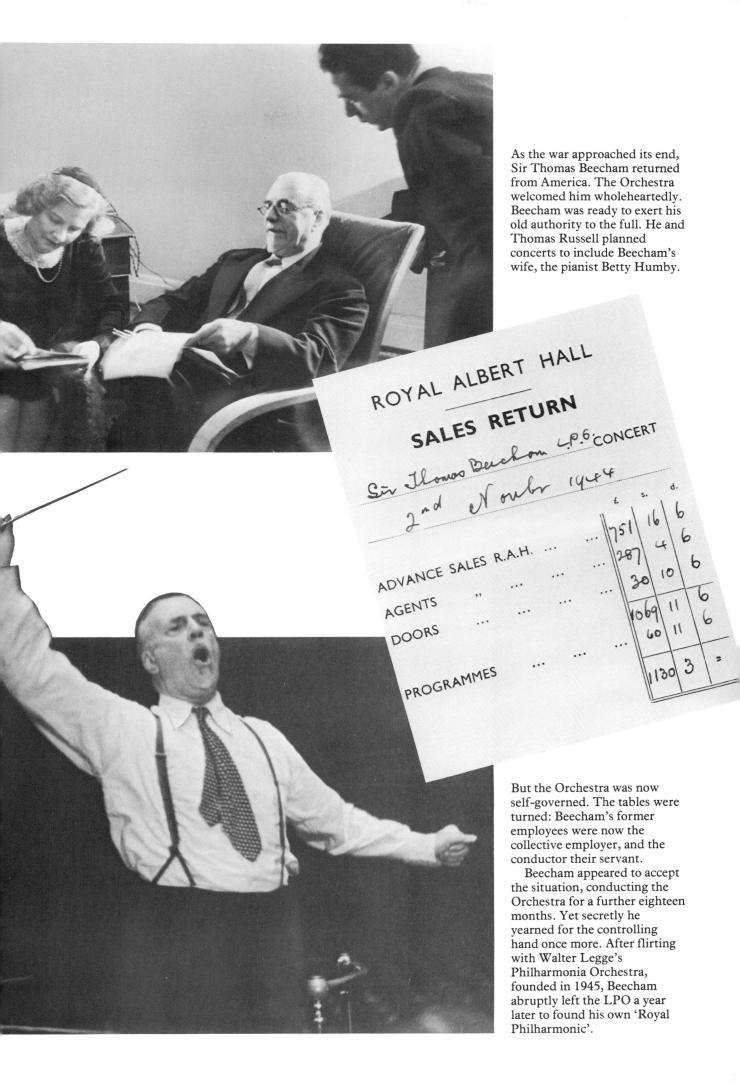

As the war approached its end, Sir Thomas Beecham returned from America. The Orchestra welcomed him wholeheartedly. Beecham was ready to exert his old authority to the full. He and Thomas Russell planned concerts to include Beecham's wife, the pianist Betty Humby.

ROYAL ALBERT HALL

SALES RETURN

Sir Thomas Beecham L.P.6. CONCERT

2nd Nov 1944

		£	s.	d.
ADVANCE SALES R.A.H.		751	16	6
AGENTS ,, ...		287	4	6
DOORS		30	10	6
		1069	11	6
		60	11	6
PROGRAMMES		1130	3	=

But the Orchestra was now self-governed. The tables were turned: Beecham's former employees were now the collective employer, and the conductor their servant.

Beecham appeared to accept the situation, conducting the Orchestra for a further eighteen months. Yet secretly he yearned for the controlling hand once more. After flirting with Walter Legge's Philharmonia Orchestra, founded in 1945, Beecham abruptly left the LPO a year later to found his own 'Royal Philharmonic'.

The postwar procession of conductors eager to conduct the LPO included Victor de Sabata.

On his arrival at Victoria Station in March 1946, de Sabata was greeted by Berta Geissmar, Felix Aprahamian and Adolph Borsdorf on behalf of the Orchestra.

De Sabata brought an intense and special dedication to his music-making. It was much needed by the Orchestra, then suffering serious exhaustion after years of wartime concert-giving in the most difficult circumstances, and from having its players poached by the two new orchestras in London.

In May 1947 de Sabata returned to conduct Beethoven's Ninth Symphony with the newly formed London Philharmonic Choir, superbly trained for the occasion by their founder-chorusmaster, Frederic Jackson.

BRUNO WALTER AT THE ALBERT HALL: *The Famous Conductor Returns to London after a Seven-Year Absence*

He left Berlin when the Nazis came to power. He was driven out of Austria, then out of Holland. For seven years he has been in the States. On his return he conducts the London Philharmonic Orchestra and is given a glowing welcome.

IN March, 1933, shortly after Bruno Walter's return from a visit to America, the musical community of Berlin became seriously concerned at a rumour that a concert of his would not take place. The rumour condensed into fact. Bruno Walter left Berlin before the date of the concert, never to return. He went to Leipzig at the urgent request of the *Gewandhaus* committee, who had telephoned him to say that "certain difficulties had arisen." As a result he conducted no more concerts there. At that time he was the Director of the Leipzig *Gewandhaus*—the famous institution of which Felix Mendelssohn had been in charge. Soon afterwards it was known that he had left Germany.

He returned to Austria. Vienna and Salzburg became the centre of his activities. He had been at home in Vienna since the years when he was assistant to Gustav Mahler at the Vienna Court Opera. From that time his relations with the Opera and the Vienna Philharmonic had always been most cordial. Salzburg gradually became the object of his utmost care, and everybody who was there at the time recalls his wonderful performances of *Orphée, Don Giovanni, Tristan, Nozze de Figaro*, and others. In 1936 Austria officially confirmed its esteem of the great musician by appointing him Artistic Director of the Vienna State Opera, so that the country and its institutions should fully benefit from his musical gifts.

In 1938, just at the moment when the world was becoming alarmed at the impending shadow over Austria, it was announced that he had been offered an extention of his contract for another three years.

CONCERT HALL TO BE

The L.C.C. have agreed to build a new concert hall as part of their South Bank development scheme, at a cost of £2,000,000.

*

ARCHITECTS

R. H. MATTHEW
(L.C.C. Architect)

J. L. MARTIN
(Deputy Architect)

EDWIN WILLIAMS, *Senior Architect*

STANLEY H. SMITH, *Principal Assistant Architect*

PETER MORO, *Associated Architect*

*

CONSULTANTS ON ACOUSTICS

HOPE BAGENAL
and the
BUILDING RESEARCH STATION

*

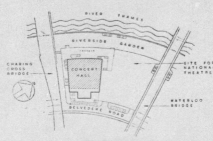

SITE PLAN
Shaded part of Concert hall to be finished by 1951.

A replacement for Queen's Hall had been discussed almost since the day of its destruction. Many wished to see it rebuilt where it had stood. But in 1946 the London County Council embarked upon a grand scheme for a complex of halls for the furtherance of all the arts on a former industrial site on the south bank of the Thames. Part of it was to become the Festival Hall.

As these plans were developing, the LCC made a £10,000 grant to the London Philharmonic Orchestra. With the contract and pension scheme devised by Thomas Russell and his committee, the LPO could now be said to be, in his words, 'the only orchestra in London (apart from the BBC) maintained on a permanent basis'. In 1947 the County Council grant was doubled.

THERE is no doubt that most people welcome the chance of putting on their best clothes and playing a tiny part in the pageant of concert or opera. Although the rules of dress have been relaxed to meet the requirements of new audiences, drawn from wider stratas of society, there is implanted in the average civilised man and woman the desire to be lords of creation once in a while and to feel that orchestras, programme sellers, bar tenders are waiting, even if mainly for mercenary reasons, upon their comfort. It has always been felt in London that only the area just north of the Thames, bounded on the east by the City, on the north by Regents Park and on the west by Kensington Gardens, qualified as the site for such pleasures as concerts, plays, operas, ballets, cabarets and eating and drinking. The South Bank would not do at all. Anyone who crossed the Thames to the Old Vic vaguely felt he was slumming, and those who indulged in some very naughty vice like visiting the Old Surrey Music Hall (long since defunct) enjoyed the sensation of being daring and sophisticated.

It has not always been so. Shakespeare was forced out of the puritanical City and played almost exclusively among the marshes of Southwark. At a later age, Sheridan and Handel were given to the élite in Vauxhall Gardens. But the Industrial Revolution certainly made a horror of most of the South Bank from Greenwich to Battersea and it is with commendable courage and imagination that the L.C.C. has set about the gigantic task of popularising a stretch of Thamesside east of the County Hall as its contribution to the 1951 Exhibition. Here will rise the Concert Hall for which London has waited so long.

A space is being cleared between County Hall and Waterloo Bridge, intercepted by the Hungerford Railway Bridge. Embankment Gardens are to be laid along the convex curve of the Thames and will be raised above the general level of the ground behind it. Thus, between the bridges, will be three levels from which the concert hall itself can be approached—the high level of Hungerford Bridge (there is also a foot bridge), the intermediary level of the Embankment Gardens, and the low level of the Belvedere Road. The concert hall group

6

It was only a short step to thinking of the new London County Council hall as an official home for its resident orchestra, the LPO. Thomas Russell took an active part in planning the new hall, and many of the planners' meetings were held at the LPO office. At the appropriate moment a feature article appeared in the *Philharmonic Post*.

MODEL OF THE CONCERT HALL

which shows the curved roof of the auditorium and how the concert hall itself has been dropped into its surrounding envelope of galleries, foyers, staircases, etc. On the left can be seen the restaurants overlooking the river.

is to rise immediately to the east of Hungerford Bridge and will comprise, in addition to a large concert hall, a smaller hall seating 700 for chamber music, amateur theatricals or school plays ; a large reception foyer for receptions, dinners and dances ; restaurants for the public ; a two-storied exhibition gallery for art displays, and two large meeting rooms. The Londoner out for a casual stroll may wander along the Embankment Gardens and refresh himself at the open air cafés with food and drink and a wonderful vista of London from the City to Westminster.

The main architectural features of the plan are quite simple to grasp. Regarding the three levels already mentioned, it is of vital importance that the most convenient point at which they can be related should prove to be the hub of this little universe. That hub is the foyer. The level of the foyer and embankment are the same. Above the foyer sits the auditorium, below it are the car parks, wash-ups, engineers' premises, and the entrances from the Belvedere Road. The foyer ceiling is the auditorium floor, and the flow of its shape, dipping down from the orchestra to the level of the conductor and sharply upwards again towards the river and the back of the auditorium, is clearly expressed. The space under the audience is wide enough towards its mouth to admit of two levels of restaurants, from the terraces of which uninterrupted views over the Thames can be enjoyed.

Having entered the concert hall by this foy up the stairs leading to the front stalls, wh may we expect to see ? Facing the orchest we will have immediately in front of us the lar marble floor which constitutes the lowest lev of the house. At the edge of this stands a podiu for the conductor. Everyone in the hall, perform and listener alike, will have an uninterrupt view of this gentleman at least down as far his coat tails. He in his turn will have forces ranged up in front of him. The first r is very shallow and wide, much shallower th we are used to in the concert halls of the pa Upon it will be seated the strings. Beyo

are the rises for woodwind, brass, percussion and choir and (though not by 1951) the concert organ. Seated, normally 100 persons can assemble confortably in the orchestra and 250 in the choir, although by bringing the strings further forward the choir can be increased to 400.

Above the orchestra and choir is a suspended ceiling. This is at once a reflector of sound and a shedder of light. It is very welcome news that such trouble is being taken over the comfort of the performers. Nothing is worse than dry acoustics against which the player works in vain, often impoverishing his own tone in his over-anxiety, or than bad light through which he has to peer at the complexities of the " Firebird." The reflector will throw back sound to the players and provide an overall diffused light. It will also have the effect for the audience of making pianissimo passages sound firm and full while remaining pianissimos. The marble floor itself which lies in front of the strings will reflect sound—particularly the tone of the strings and the soloists.

If we turn our backs on the performing end of the concert hall we will find ourselves in a rectangular shaped room with the seats rising steadily and quite steeply towards the rear of the auditorium. A gallery projects forward at the same angle as the floor and the ceiling correspondingly rises in height towards the back. It is rather amusing to reflect that after

The London County Council sponsored the Orchestra in a comprehensive series of children's concerts. The conductor was Dr Leslie Russell (right), shown here in a typical moment after a concert with the Orchestra's principal trumpet, Eric Bravington (signing autographs).

Many outstanding conductors visited the LPO during the postwar years. Among the young men were Georg Solti (above left) and Sergiu Celibidache (below left, with members of the Orchestra listening to a recording playback in a room behind the platform at Kingsway Hall). One of the most faithful of the older generation was Basil Cameron (above right, with the leader in 1946, James Andrew Cooper). Cameron had conducted concerts with the Orchestra almost from its inception, and had shared the most arduous wartime tours with Sargent. Another visitor of the older generation was Furtwängler. Where Bruno Walter had fled from Nazism, Furtwängler had remained to try to carry on music in his native country, despite politics rather than because of them. His postwar appearance with the LPO showed that this was generally understood.

At last the Orchestra's search for a permanent conductor seemed to have been solved in the happiest way – in the person of Eduard van Beinum, who had conducted occasional concerts with the Orchestra since 1946. He brought to the LPO a breadth of spirit and of repertoire which combined with a superb rehearsal technique to raise the standard of playing to heights unknown since Beecham's days.

The Directors of the
LONDON PHILHARMONIC ORCHESTRA
have pleasure in inviting you to meet

EDUARD
VAN BEINUM

at a Reception in honour of his appointment as
Principal Conductor

on

Monday, January 24th, 1949
5 – 7 p.m.
at 53 Welbeck Street, W.1

R.S.V.P. to
Secretary,
53 Welbeck Street, W.1

Van Beinum and Thomas Russell found immediate understanding and formed a close working relationship.

Four stages in preparing a concert, *c*.1950:

1. Van Beinum plans the Orchestra's schedule with Thomas Russell and Adolph Borsdorf.
2. The *Philharmonic Post* assistant editor, Alan Gregory, organizes publicity.
3. The public purchase their tickets.
4. The Albert Hall audience await the Orchestra's entry.

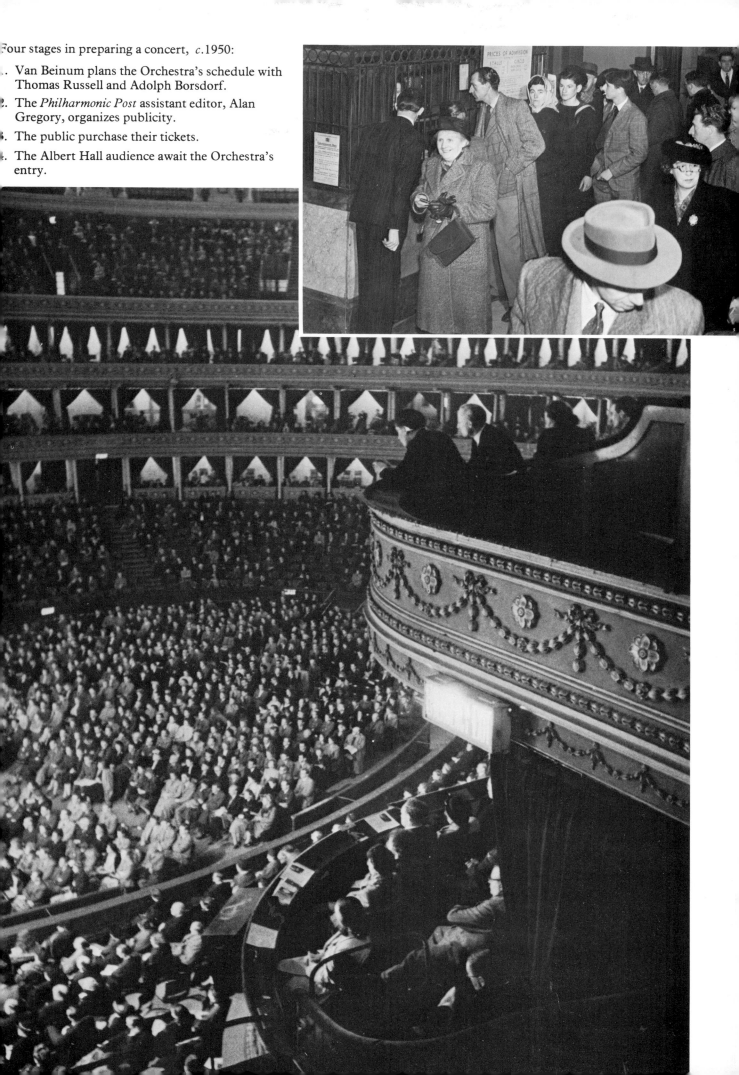

In the postwar years the Orchestra frequently toured Western Europe.

The London Philharmonic Orchestra

ON TOUR

In May 1950, during a tour of Belgium and Holland, the LPO reached Arnhem, where hundreds of British soldiers had perished in the Second World War. At the monument erected on the centre of the battlefield, a wreath was laid on behalf of the Orchestra by the sub-leader, Howard Leyton-Brown, who had been an ace RAF bomber pilot in the war.

Orchestra still
resident principal
tor. Early in 1950,
ian Boult reached the
sory retiring age set
BBC. Here was the
lution to van
's enforced absence
declining health.
ook over as principal
tor.

952: the Orchestra's
pearance on
on, with Sir Adrian
'The Conductor

Thomas Russell had grown up the son of a poor family. In his youth he had watched a beloved elder brother's slow death from the effects of gas in the First World War. He had come to feel that the economic and military bases of Western society were wrong. In the 1930s the Spanish Civil War turned him towards Communism. He made no secret of his sympathy, but maintained that it was a private matter.

The years after the Second World War saw a rising fear of Communism. Russell had secured the London County Council's annual grant for the LPO – since 1948 £25,000 *per annum* – despite the LPO's reputation as 'the

Red Orchestra'. In the McCarthy era, this was a poten source of official embarrassment. When Russell was invite to Moscow in 1949, he decided to go as a private person, bu *The Daily Worker* reported the affair with the Orchestra' name in its headlines.

As a result the LCC announced the withdrawal of its annua grant to the Orchestra. It also withdrew the understanding tha the LPO would be the resident orchestra at its new hall (to b opened at the Festival of Britain in 1951), announcing that th Royal Festival Hall would be available to all the Londo orchestras without preference.

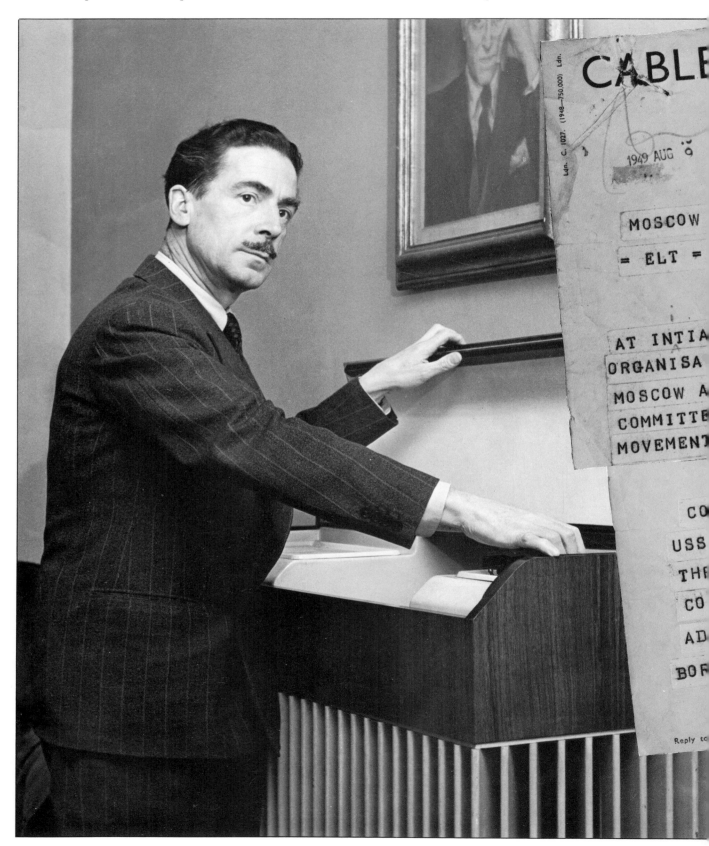

Over the years the London Philharmonic Orchestra had remained loyal to the man who had been secretary since 1939, and chairman and managing director since 1945. It was not too much to say that the Orchestra owed its very survival to Russell's dogged courage and rigorous, informed advocacy.

But in 1952 Russell accepted an invitation to visit the People's Republic of China. At this, great pressure was applied to the Orchestra from outside its ranks to dismiss him. In November 1952 a full meeting of the Orchestra voted the dismissal. The vote was close, and several members of the Orchestra resigned in protest.

M VIA NORTHERN

REAT NORTHERN TELEGRAPH CO.

(LIMITED) OF DENMARK

LONDON 9 AU C.T.C. L 154

10 0044 NORTHERN

JSSELL C/O SCR 14 KENSINGTON SQUARE

LONDON/W=8 =

OVIET PUBLIC TRADEUNION AND CULTURAL
UNION PEACE CONFERENCE BEING CONVENED
NTY FIFTH STOP BEHALF ORGANISATIONAL
YOU AS ACTIVE PARTICIPANT PEACE
AT CONFERENCE STOP YOUR PRESENCE AT

Cablegrams "VIA NORTHERN" will also be accepted by any Post Office.

GN
WILL BE NEW PROOF COMMON EFFORTS PEOPLES
TAIN ENSURE DURABLE AND LASTING PEACE
WORLD STOP PLEASE INFORM US EARLIEST
DATE YOUR ... VAL FOLLOWING
... TOP ACADEMICIAN
KROPOTKIN ... MMITTEE

or messengers, enq

ORCHESTRA'S COMMUNIST CHIEF GOES

4 RESIGN AFTER L.P.O. DISMISSAL

"WITCH HUNT VICTIM" CLAIM

From Our SPECIAL CORRESPONDENT
CHISLEHURST, Kent, Sunday.

Mr. Thomas Russell, 50, chairman and managing director of the London Philharmonic Orchestra, has been relieved of his post by a majority vote of the shareholders. He has been a member of the Communist party for 16 years.

At his home here to-night he said to me that he felt he had been "the victim of a witch-hunt." As a protest against his dismissal, four other members of the orchestra's permanent staff, including his secretary, have resigned.

One of them is Mr. Adolf Borsdof, who has been concert director for 10 years. Mr. Borsdof, who is not a Communist, said:

"I resigned because I was disgusted with the way the campaign against Mr. Russell had been conducted. Also I had no confidence in the future administration. I was pressed to stay on, but I refused."

HAD LETTER IN PEKING

Last August Mr. Russell was in a British delegation, including four Socialist M.P.s, which visited Communist China. On Sept. 28, while in Peking, he received a letter asking him to resign.

When he returned home early in October he met the directors. He told them he would refuse to resign.

Shareholders later received a letter signed by Sir Adrian Boult, the orchestra's conductor. Thirteen of them, members of the orchestra, replied, asking Sir Adrian to substantiate points he had made.

On Nov. 14, at a full meeting of the shareholders, a proposition that Mr. Russell be relieved of his post was carried by 27 votes to 22 with one abstention. Mr. Russell said to-night:

"Although I feel I have been the victim of a witch-hunt, this is not the important issue. For 13 years the orchestra has been a happy combination of self-governing players who have now, by a misguided action, handed over the essential part of their administration to outside influences.

"Only in this way can Sir Adrian's letter be explained. I am sure that only extreme pressure from outside would have led him to take such a step. I left the orchestra in the most favourable financial position it has enjoyed since its foundation in 1932."

After saying that he had been a friend of Sir Adrian's for about 15 years, Mr. Russell added: "I feel that the demand for my resignation was connected with my visit to China, although the board agreed to my going there on my holidays.

"Some people seem to think I went against my will, because the Communist party ordered me. This is nonsense. No one has ever attempted to tell me what I should or not do in my work.

"In the past 13 years we have had our disagreements in the orchestra. But they have always been settled and there has not been a happier orchestra in the country.

"Now there are two separate fac-tions. Suggestions of a Communist

The management of the Orchestra was reorganized with the appointment of a general administrator, Thomas O'Dea. The new chairman was the principal trumpet, Eric Bravington.

In October 1953 the Orchestra celebrated its twenty-first birthday with a concert and party for old and new members and friends at the Royal Albert Hall. Malcolm Arnold, the Orchestra's former principal trumpet, wrote a *Flourish for a Twenty-First Birthday* and Vaughan Williams conducted his *Serenade to Music* with the London Philharmonic Choir and Orchestra.

Dr. Vaughan Williams conducting his 'Serenade to Music' at the Royal Albert Hall on October 7th

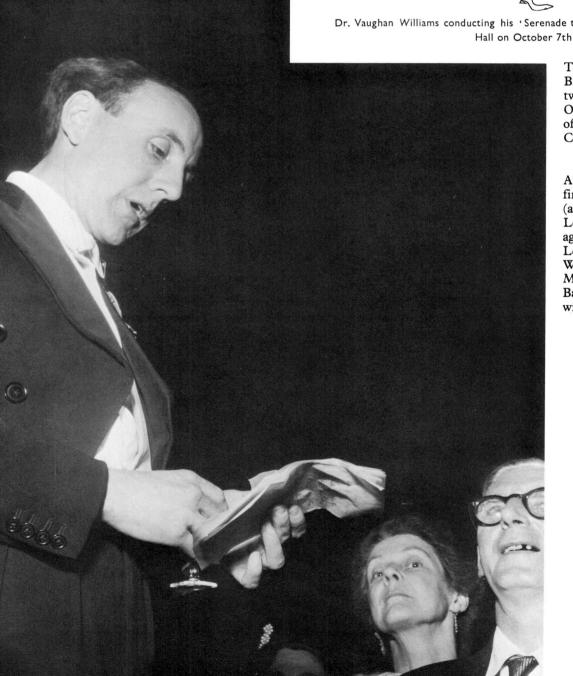

The chairman, Eric Bravington, reading the twenty-first birthday address. On the right is Isaac Hayward of the London County Council.

At the Orchestra's twenty-first birthday celebration: (above, left to right) Mrs Leon Goossens, the concert agent Mrs Emmie Tillett, Leon Goossens, Maurice Ward, Mr and Mrs Algy McCordall; (below) George Barker of the Orchestra's staff with Sir Arthur Bliss.

The 'ideas man' on the Orchestra's staff was George Barker. He wrote:

A new spirit was abroad. In thinking out new ways of gaining converts to music, we realized that w[e] had to do more than put up concerts in the old way. . . . We had to integrate our work with the life of th[e] community. . . .

On a summer evening [in 1952] three of us were standing in the nave of Thaxted Parish Church[,] the Vicar of Thaxted, the concert director of the London Philharmonic Orchestra, and myself. . .[.] Out of such a chance encounter sprang a new chapter in the history of concert giving in this country[.]

Two months later Thaxted Church was full to overflowing with people listening to the Londo[n] Philharmonic Orchestra. . . .

Music makes its deepest impression on persons when they are in a mood to receive it, and associatio[n] is an invaluable aid to such a mood. Who will ever forget the first chord of the Tallis Fantasia, *wh[o] has heard it against the background of a Dedham or Long Melford choir? To musicians it is the chor[d] of G major, to us who listen it is the entry into another world.*

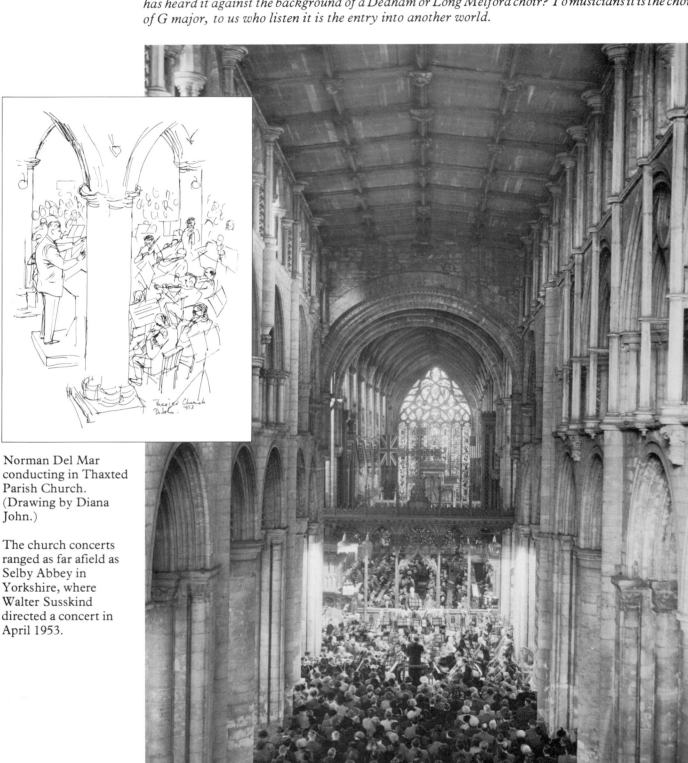

Norman Del Mar conducting in Thaxted Parish Church. (Drawing by Diana John.)

The church concerts ranged as far afield as Selby Abbey in Yorkshire, where Walter Susskind directed a concert in April 1953.

In a time of increasing financial difficulty, gramophone recording played a vital role in the Orchestra's activities. A valuable contract for many recordings was made with the Nixa Company and its American affiliate, Westminster. One of the most successful results was Walton's *Belshazzar's Feast*. The record was made at Walthamstow Assembly Hall in September 1953 with the great British baritone Dennis Noble, the London Philharmonic Choir and Orchestra under the direction of Sir Adrian Boult.

A point of balance: Nixa's recording director Dr Kurt List (right) conferring with Sir Adrian and the Orchestra's librarian, Jack Jones.

In December 1953 the Orchestra completed recording for
Decca all Vaughan Williams's symphonies, under the
supervision of the composer. It was a milestone in the
history of British music and of gramophone recording. The
Decca sessions took place in Kingsway Hall, under Sir
Adrian Boult, with the composer and his wife Ursula (left
rear) in constant attendance. Vaughan Williams gave the
Orchestra generous praise, and some of his observations
were included on one of the discs.

Ursula Vaughan Williams recalled:

*It was both tedious and exhilarating: tedious in the gaps
and waits, the murky, greenish blue tipped-up seats, the
rumble of trains passing under the hall and disorganizing
the music, the cold weather and the sandwich meals:
exhilarating in the concentration, the repetition of each
passage, first live, then recorded, then live again, with
hearing sharpened to take in every variation of clarity,
balance and tempo. It was a lesson in musical structure, as
well as in professional concentration, to watch composer,
conductor and players listening critically to every detail of
their work as it came back from the machine while the live
sound was fresh in their ears.* [21]

In 1956, with the support of the British Council, the LPO became the first Western orchestra to visit Russia. Sir Adrian Boult, still principal conductor at sixty-seven, decided, however, that he must remain at home; the Orchestra sought a substitute conductor for the tour. Sir Adrian recalled:

Two or three weeks before zero hour . . . a strange young man from the Soviet Cultural Attaché's department called at Welbeck Street and asked numerous questions. . . . He asked to see the programmes and, noting the absence of my name, asked why was not I going. The answer had to be that 'Moscow knew six months ago. . . .' His reply was true to Soviet technique: 'Oh, but if Boult does not go I think I shall have to cancel the whole trip.'

No one had any idea how far this gentleman was bluffing, but an alarmed meeting of the British Council, Arts Council and general administrator waylaid me immediately afterwards. This was followed by a summons to the Foreign Office and the exercise of all Lord Reading's persuasive powers. I did not see how I could risk being the cause of this cancellation. It would almost certainly spell the bankruptcy of the LPO, and so my wife and I began to plan how to go to Moscow by train. [22]

The LPO under Sir
Adrian Boult (above)
giving a concert in the
Great Hall of Moscow
Conservatory.

The Russian conductor
Yevgeni Mravinski, Sir
Adrian, Dmitri
Shostakovich, Igor
Oistrakh and Aram
Khachaturian.

The violinist David
Oistrakh introducing
his son Igor through an
interpreter to Sir
Adrian.

After the Russian tour, Sir
Adrian Boult decided he must
retire as principal conductor,
though he continued to work
with the Orchestra
frequently. Through the late
1950s many conductors
visited, including Constantin
Silvestri (above) and Josef
Krips.

These were bad years for orchestral finance. By 1957, with an accumulated deficit of £38,000, another major reorganization was needed. It was draconian: fixed salaries were eliminated, the members were once more paid by engagement, and the Orchestra itself undertook no further concert promotion for the time being. All this meant that the LPO was no longer a contract orchestra. Paid holidays were eliminated, the pension fund wound up, and the administrative staff reduced from fourteen to eight. Among the losses was the position of general administrator.

The general administrator's duties were taken over by the chairman, Eric Bravington, who continued as the Orchestra's principal trumpet while he shouldered the Herculean task of running the LPO office with its severely reduced staff. In 1959 he produced a plan for a 'London Philharmonic Society'.

LONDON PHILHARMONIC SOCIETY

General

It is becoming increasingly clear that planned concert giving is essential to London's musical life. At the present time competition between impresarios and other concert promoters is tending to produce stereotyped programmes, often inadequately rehearsed and usually given at irregular intervals – a state of affairs which is creating bewilderment amongst the London musical public.

Consequent upon the success of the concerts given by the London Philharmonic Orchestra in its Historical and other series it has become apparent that there is a precedent for the planning of musical activities to ensure the building up of an intelligent and experienced audience, such as has been found possible in other important capitals.

Proposal

It is proposed to form a non-profit distributing company registered as a charity, to be known as

    "London Philharmonic Society".

Whilst the immediate objective would be to promote three important series of orchestral concerts at the Royal Festival Hall in the season 1959/60, at the earliest possible moment it would be hoped to extend the activities of the Society to cover wider aspects of music making in London, such as a series of recitals and a chamber music series. Tickets for all the Society's concerts will be reasonably inexpensive in order to attract a wide public.

Constitution

The Society would be governed by a board of Directors made up of those sponsoring this proposal and others eminent in various walks of London life, making a total of about thirty persons to be known as the Council of the Society.

The Council would be divided into:

    A Programme Committee
    A Finance Committee
    A General Purposes and Publicity Committee

The Chairman of the Council and Chairmen of the Committees would form an Executive Committee to settle urgent and important matters.

            1.

The measures devised by Bravington and his board gradually brought the Orchestra out of its deepest crisis since 1940. When Eric Bravington was forced to retire as a playing member following an illness in 1959, the Orchestra immediately made him managing director – a position which he was to occupy with distinction for more than twenty years.

Through the darkest days of financial crisis the Arts Council carefully monitored the situation. Grants were made for concerts outside London. The London County Council made possible a series of concerts in the environs of London. Among the happiest, when the weather permitted, were performances in the new shell at Kenwood House on

In 1958 the Orchestra appointed a new permanent conductor, William Steinberg. His strength as an interpreter was matched by his energy in orchestral drilling, and he worked hard to improve playing standards. The Orchestra toured up and down the country, much as they had done during the war and immediately after: here they are seen at Grimsby.

But Steinberg was almost sixty at the time of his appointment, and his continuing interests in the United States necessitated constant travel. Within two years the LPO was forced again to search for a permanent conductor.

Much needed relief and relaxation were found in the LPO cricket team, ever hopeful and sensationally unsuccessful.

Early in 1962 the Orchestra undertook its first tour of India, Australia and the Far East. Conducting was shared between the talented young John Pritchard and the Orchestra's old friend, Sir Malcolm Sargent.

Arrival at Bombay, 25 February 1962: Sir Malcolm Sargent and Eric Bravington being welcomed by Indian officials.

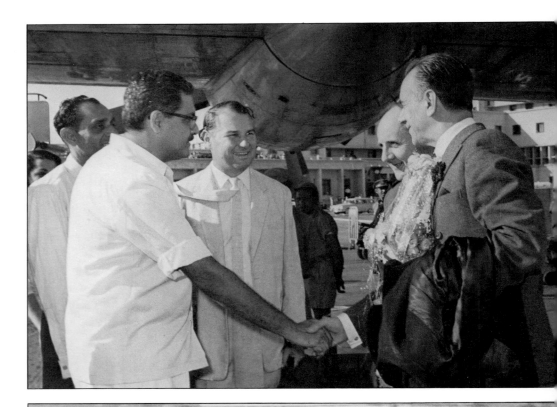

A strenuous rehearsa

Guests for the Orchestra's
concert at Vigyan Bhavan, 1
March 1962: Jawaharlal
Nehru, Mr and Mrs Croom-
Johnson (representing the
British Council, sponsors of
the tour) and Mrs Indira
Gandhi.

GREETINGS TELEGRAM

E250 GTG 4.2 PM KNIGHTSBRIDGE 33/34=

GREETING-MR JOHN PRITCHARD FESTHALL SEDIST LONDON=

MY SINCEREST GOOD WISHES TO YOU AND ALL MEMBERS OF THE LPO

MAY YOU HAVE A HAPPY AND SUCCESSFUL SEASON THE FORERUNNER OF

MANY TOGETHER= MALCOLM SARGENT+ +

In 1962 the Orchestra found its next permanent conductor and artistic director in John Pritchard. His years remain in the memory of one LPO player as an era of 'supreme good taste' in the Orchestra's music-making.

In 1963 the London Philharmonic Choir and Orchestra received a visit from the eighty-six-year-old Pablo Casals, who conducted the British premiere of his oratorio *El Pessebre (The Manger)*. After the concert, Eric Bravington made a presentation to Casals.

Among the members of the Orchestra was Marie Wilson – the first woman member aside from harpists, and one of the best known and most popular of London orchestral violinists. Nearly twenty years later, now in her late seventies, she is still with the LPO.

In 1964 the LPO was invited to become resident orchestra for the summer festival of opera at Glyndebourne, where John Pritchard was principal conductor. It remains the Orchestra's principal summer engagement and has proved an extremely fruitful partnership, providing a unique quality to the music of the performances and at the same time adding a valuable dimension to the Orchestra's repertoire.

In the Organ Room at Glyndebourne, Raymond Leppard directed members of the LPO in a recording of Cavalli's *L'Ormindo*, produced in the adjoining opera house in 1967 and 1968.

A Glyndebourne dress rehearsal of Mozart's *Don Giovanni*.

The end of the 1969 Glyndebourne season: George Christie (son of Glyndebourne's founder) and his wife saying goodbye to violinists of the Orchestra (from left) Sergei Bezkorvany, John Kuchmy, Dennis Simons and (right) Marie Wilson.

At home: To the Orchestra's delight Sir Adrian Boult accepted the title of President in 1965. Through the 1960s and 1970s Sir Adrian enjoyed an Indian summer, conducting many LPO concerts and making a long series of important records with the Orchestra.

Abroad: Touring in Germany and Austria, 1966. The effects of the Second World War were still clear after more than twenty years.

One source of income came from films. Here the Orchestra is recording Bernard Herrmann's score for the Czech film *The Battle of Neretva*. The sessions, in December 1969 under the direction of the composer, established the mood and atmosphere of the film as well as matching the music precisely to the film's action.

Keith Whitmore, the Orchestra's principal horn and chairman of the board, playing a Mozart concerto in October 1965 under Anatole Fistoulari. After a brief time as a principal conductor in the early 1940s, Fistoulari often conducted the Orchestra.

Yehudi Menuhin celebrated his fiftieth birthday in a special concert with the Orchestra at the Festival Hall on 26 April 1966. In the photograph he is shown rehearsing Mozart's *Concerto for Three Pianos* with his sisters Hephzibah and Yaltah and his son Jeremy. The event was recorded and filmed for television.

Gradually the Orchestra's financial problems were being solved. There remained the artistic problem of playing standards which had never fully recovered their prewar brilliance. In 1967 the LPO appointed a new principal conductor and artistic director. He was Bernard Haitink, one of the world's most dynamic and talented young musicians. In a sense, Haitink's relationship with the LPO went back more than a decade, for he was the protégé of Eduard van Beinum.

Rosalie Cody, the Orchestra's concerts manager, planning future schedules with Eric Bravington.

Haitink began to raise the Orchestra's playing standards, first to match those of the Beecham era and ultimately to exceed them. His tenure was to last longer than that of any other principal conductor in LPO history – twelve years.

One notable LPO recording under Haitink was of Dvořák's *Cello Concerto and Rondo* (in November 1967). The soloist, Maurice Gendron, had the opportunity of going over both works with the composer's daughter-in-law, Mme Julie Dvořákova. The Philips recording took advantage of the latest techniques of multi-channel microphoning, with the level of each separately controlled from the console 'mixer'.

One important way of raising money and gaining publicity is the Orchestra's National Appeal Fund concerts, some of which have starred leading figures in the light entertainment world. In 1966 Danny Kaye conducted the Orchestra in a programme which included Rossini's *Thieving Magpie* Overture and Johann Strauss's *Tritsch-Tratsch* Polka.

In 1967 the guest was Duke Ellington, seen here with the Orchestra's leader Rodney Friend (the youngest leader in the Orchestra's history when he was appointed in 1964 at the age of twenty-four).

The tables were turned in 1969,
when the Orchestra was invited to
appear on the Jack Benny Show.

In 1971, to celebrate the centenary
of the Royal Albert Hall, the
Orchestra was conducted by
Robert Farnon in a programme
entitled 'Get Happy with the
LPO'. The special guest was Tony
Bennett, and the hall was sold out.

The London Philharmonic established the London Philharmonic Society (USA) Inc. to assist in financing American tours. The Orchestra made its first United States tours in 1970 and 1971. The last stage in the complex preparations saw the Orchestra's tours manager, Jean Stephenson, double-checking the shipment of instruments at Heathrow.

At Old Tucson: Derek James (principal trombone), Stephen Crabtree (co-principal double bass), Peter Vel (cello), Allan McDougall (viola) and David Strange (cello).

The 1971 USA tour included a visit to the West Coast, with coach travel through the California desert.

Erich Leinsdorf conducting the
Orchestra in California.

In 1973 the LPO toured China – the first Western orchestra to visit the People's Republic – laying the foundations for the fruitful cultural exchanges of more recent years. The visit was also celebrated in a BBC television programme entitled 'The Red Carpet' which was very well received.

Among the first off the plane were the Orchestra's chairman, Keith Whitmore (left) and Eric Bravington.

Chinese hospitality included a visit to the giant pandas at Canton Zoo.

During a river cruise from Shanghai, the Orchestra listened to a children's violin ensemble.

欢迎英国伦敦爱乐管弦乐团访华演出

'A WARM WELCOME TO THE LONDON PHILHARMONIC ORCHESTRA ON THEIR TOUR OF CHINA'
read the banner over the platform at Canton. Local and regional leaders lined the platform to greet the Orchestra, the
tour conductor, John Pritchard, and the Earl of Shaftesbury, Chairman of the LPO Council (front row, sixth from right).

On the Great Wall.

For years the LPO had had to rehearse in many different halls. Providing an adequate rehearsal facility was one clear way of relieving pressure on seriously overworked players. A survey of redundant churches in London suggested that Holy Trinity, Southwark, might meet the need.

On 10 December 1972, John Pritchard conducted the LPO in acoustical tests in the draughty, dilapidated church, the players wearing tin hats to protect them against the risk of falling plaster. The tests were successful, and the LPO together with the London Symphony Orchestra determined to raise the money – in the end £650,000 – to equip Holy Trinity as their rehearsal hall. The Orchestra offered grateful thanks to Lord Shaftesbury and all the other people involved for their valuable work in raising the necessary funds.

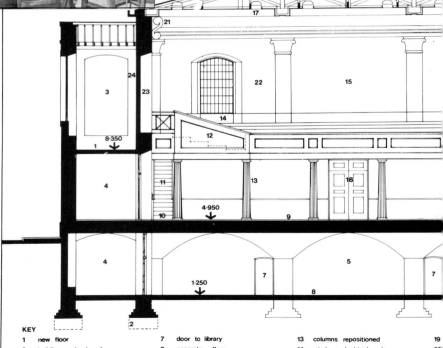

KEY

1	new floor	7	door to library	13	columns repositioned	19
2	building underpinned	8	concrete floor	14	windows doubleglazed	20
3	boiler room and water storage	9	timber and stone floor	15	position of organ	21
4	lobby	10	perimeter supply air duct in floor	16	air extract through tower	22
5	cafeteria	11	new stair to gallery	17	air extract through light fittings	23
6	door to conductor's room	12	side galleries modified	18	door to recording rooms	24

n the early hours of 1 October 1973
– the very day the building work was
o begin – fire swept through the
mpty structure.

nough of the building remained to
arry on with the project. A
ubstantial donation from the Henry
Vood Memorial Trust determined
he naming of the new hall after the
edoubtable founder of the Proms,
ho had conducted both the LPO
nd LSO.

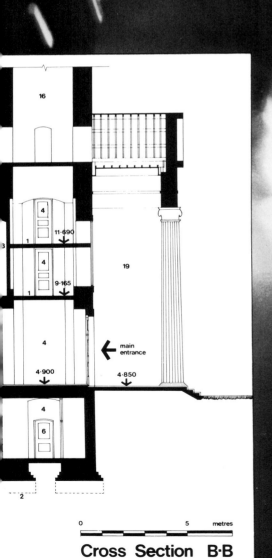

Cross Section B·B

In June 1975 the Henry Wood Hall was ready, and the LPO
with Bernard Haitink could enjoy adequate, assured rehearsal
space for the first time.

Throughout the tour, Bravingto[n]
worked tirelessly. For services [to]
music he was awarded the OBE i[n]
the 1973 Birthday Honour[s]

A Continental tour in the autumn of
1973 took the Orchestra to Vienna. The
busy, demanding schedule worked out
by Eric Bravington and his experienced
office team still allowed time for visits,
grave (principal double bass William
Webster at the Mozart monument) and
light-hearted (Derek James at the
Musikverein).

At the Edinburgh Festival, 1974, Carlo Maria Giulini conducted the Verdi *Requiem* with Rita Hunter, Fiorenza Cossotto, Luciano Pavarotti and Raffaele Arié. The Orchestra had appeared at the Edinburgh Festivals since the early 1950s.

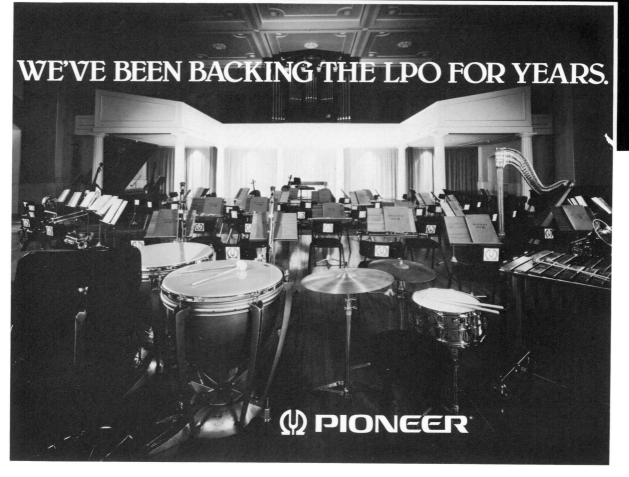

LAMBERT & BUTLER

As part of W.D. & H.O. Wills, Lambert & Butler are pleased to be continuing the Company's 15-year association with the London Philharmonic Orchestra.

The London Philharmonic Orchestra have made more than 50 recordings on the Lambert & Butler Master Series of classical recordings. Sales exceed 2¼ million and the budget price records can be purchased from all major dealers.

LAMBERT & BUTLER
MASTER
SERIES

For many years the Orchestra has received vital support from the Arts Council of Great Britain and Greater London Council, through the London Orchestral Concerts Board. In the 1960s industrial and commercial companies began to make important contributions to the Orchestra's existence. The advertisements they generated have made distinctive additions to LPO programmes.

Commercial Union Assurance
London Philharmonic Orchestra

Conductor Bernard Haitink

Liverpool
Philharmonic Hall March 4

Manchester
Free Trade Hall March 5

Derby
Assembly Rooms March 6

Nottingham
Albert Hall March 7

CU Assurance

RUSSIA, 1975

A second Russian visit took the Orchestra, under Bernard Haitink, to Moscow and Leningrad.

Russian diplomacy . . .

UNITED STATES, 1976

Another American tour marked the bicentenary of the United States.

... and American.

Bernard Haitink was created an honorary KBE in October 1977, shortly before the tenth anniversary of his first concert as principal conductor of the LPO. But Haitink's appointment as musical director at Glyndebourne (together with his concurrent responsibility for the Concertgebouw Orchestra) forced him to stand down from the LPO conductorship at the end of the 1978–79 season.

6 July 1977. At the Orchestra's Festival Hall concert to celebrate the Royal Silver Jubilee, Her Majesty Queen Elizabeth, the Queen Mother, met Sir Georg and Lady Solti. In the background were John Denison, a member of the LPO Council (centre), and the Orchestra's chairman, Stephen Crabtree (right). In 1979 Sir Georg became the LPO's principal conductor.

David James (double bass).

Artists' courtyard buffet during rehearsal break.

John Pritchard conducting a Glyndebourne recording for Southern Television.

The stage band in *Don Giovanni*.

The youngest of the leading conductors who appeared regularly with the LPO in the 1970s was Daniel Barenboim. Even then his association with the Orchestra was nearly twenty years old, for he had appeared as piano soloist in a concert conducted by Sir Adrian Boult in 1958. Eighteen years later he was rehearsing the LPO at Henry Wood Hall for their London concerts.

Sir Adrian's distinguished career in music-making, which spanned almost sixty-five years, came to an end in December 1978 (some twenty-eight years after his retirement by the BBC) with his last recording session conducting the LPO. The recording was of music by Sir Hubert Parry, who had befriended Adrian Boult in the early 1900s. In April 1979 the LPO gave two concerts to celebrate Sir Adrian's ninetieth birthday

On 5 June 1979 the Orchestra and Choir participated in a unique event – a concert at the Royal Festival Hall to celebrate the hundredth birthday of Sir Robert Mayer. Sir Robert had been one of Beecham's original guarantors in founding the London Philharmonic Orchestra nearly half a century earlier and the Children's Concerts he had sponsored with the Orchestra had evolved into the world-famous 'Youth and Music' programme.

The works in the concert were all chosen by Sir Robert Mayer himself. One was Berlioz's *Nuits d'été*, conducted by Sir Colin Davis with Dame Janet Baker as soloist.

The concert was attended by Her Majesty the Queen, the Duke of Edinburgh and the Prince of Wales. During the interval, Her Majesty made Sir Robert a Knight Commander of the Royal Victorian Order.

When the great Russian cellist Mstislav Rostropovich turned to conducting, the Orchestra quickly recognized a formidable new talent. Here he is shown in the recording studio listening to a playback with the EMI producer Suvi Raj Grubb and members of the Orchestra: (from the left) David Theodore (principal oboe), David Nolan (leader), Martin Parry (principal flute) and Russell Gilbert (principal second violin).

Rostropovich's prowess as a conductor was nearly matched by his eminence as a fracturer of the English language. At a press luncheon to launch his LPO recording of the complete Tchaikovsky symphonies, he asked that there be only brief recorded extracts before lunch:
'Critics not so angry if good eat before!'

In 1979 the LPO won an important appeal and made legal history. A member whose engagement had been terminated took the Orchestra to court, claiming that he was an employee and had been unfairly dismissed. The case turned upon the question of whether the Orchestra was an 'employer'. The Orchestra stated that its musicians were self-employed, and therefore not subject to the existing employment legislation. This view was upheld by an Industrial Tribunal and the Employment Appeal Tribunal.

In a later case the LPO – acting on behalf of itself, the London Symphony, the Philharmonia and the Royal Philharmonic Orchestras – established that its extra players were also self-employed.

These two decisions went far beyond the specific interests of players and orchestra. Had it been ruled that the LPO was an 'employer', the Department of Health and Social Security would have required National Insurance contributions of all orchestra players at employee rates, and the Inland Revenue would have required all orchestras to operate a Pay-As-You-Earn system. The resulting financial burden, added to the other problems of running contract orchestras, would effectively have stopped a great proportion of music-making in London. It might well have meant the end of a supreme era in British music.

that the law can be that whether what was agreed between Mr. Winfield and the company fits the legal concept of " contract of service," or not, **A** can be a question of law if the agreement is reduced to a formal document but a question of fact if it is not. Happily we do not have to decide this question. If it were open to us to say whether in our judgment the industrial tribunal was right in its decision, we would have no hesitation in saying that it was.

As has often been pointed out, it can be very difficult to decide whether **B** a relationship between employer and employee is a contract of service. A helpful analysis of considerations is set out in *Ready Mixed Concrete (South East) Ltd.* v. *Minister of Pensions and National Insurance* [1968] 2 Q.B. 497. But, like all decisions, that has to be read in its context, and the question in this case has to be considered not in the normal industrial or commercial context, but in the context of one of the world's finest orchestras composed of some of the world's finest musicians. Making **C** music is an art, and the co-operation required for a performance of Berlioz's Requiem is dissimilar to that required between the manufacturer of concrete and the truck driver who takes the concrete where it is needed.

If our only power to entertain this appeal is on the alternative basis that the question decided by the industrial tribunal was a question of fact, then the submission is that the tribunal erred in law in that it misconceived **D** the position of the members of the L.P.O. as shareholders in the company, that it relied on inadmissible opinion evidence on the nature of the relationship of members with the company, and that the decision was one that no sensible tribunal properly directing itself could have reached.

In our judgment the industrial tribunal correctly addressed itself to the reality of the situation. It took the view, as we think it was entitled **E** on the material before it to do, that the company was simply machinery through which the members of the orchestra managed and controlled the orchestra's operation. No doubt it regarded the " gentleman's agreement " reference in the memorandum as significant. Relatively little of the evidence pointed to the sort of relationship under which Mr. Winfield had served Western Orchestral Society Ltd. Much pointed to a co-operative **F** association between artistes who must subject themselves to self-discipline in order that the result of the operation, the making of orchestral music, can be achieved. We think that if an officious bystander, at any time between May 15, 1968, and July 6, 1978, had said to Mr. Winfield " Who is your employer?," whatever answer a lawyer might have given, he, the artiste, would have said " We don't have a boss, we run ourselves through **G** a company, and we hire eleven administrators to do it."

That was in effect the view the industrial tribunal took. In our judgment they were entitled to look, as they did, to the reality of the matter; and they were entitled on the material before them to reach the conclusion which they did. In deciding whether you are in the presence of a contract of service or not you look at the whole of the picture. **H** This picture looks to us, as it looked to the industrial tribunal, like a co-operative of distinguished musicians running themselves with self and mutual discipline, and in no sense like a boss and his musician employees. In our judgment the industrial tribunal did not fall into an error of law, either in their approach or their conclusion, and the appeal is dismissed.

Appeal dismissed.

Solicitors: *Lawford & Co.; Charles Russell & Co.*

John Cobb, the Orchestra's personnel manager, 1972–80.

'The compleat bassist's kit', 1978.

In April 1980 the Orchestra and Choir mounted a performance of the Berlioz *Requiem (Grande Messe des Morts)* in the Festival Hall, followed by a recording. The conductor was André Previn, appearing with the Orchestra for the first time.

The recording, in Walthamstow Assembly Hall, was produced for EMI by Suvi Raj Grubb, who wrote:

The Grande Messe *was written . . . with extra horns, tenor drum, bass drum, tam tams, cymbals, five extra timpanists (each with three instruments) and four brass bands of cornets, trumpets, trombones and tuba. . . .*

Berlioz asks that band one should be at the north, two to the east, three to the west and four to the south. . . .

At the end of the sessions when we thanked the staff of the Hall and said we hoped we had not been too much trouble, they replied:

'Oh no, you were nice to work with – but, by God, we have never heard anyone before produce so much sound.' [23]

In 1980 Eric Bravington retired after twenty years as the Orchestra's managing director. The length of his service to the Orchestra and the continuity of his management was unequalled in the annals of London orchestras. To mark their gratitude, the Orchestra and Sir Georg Solti made presentations to him at their concert in the Royal Festival Hall on 7 December 1980.

Eric Bravington's successor as managing director, Stephen Crabtree (carrying on the tradition of having risen from the ranks of the players), looked on with members of the Orchestra as Sir Georg Solti presented the baton with which he had just opened the 1980–81 season to the LPO's patron, His Royal Highness the Duke of Kent.

The Orchestra's chairman and principal horn, Nicholas Busch (right),
with the LPO horns, (from left) Iain Keddie, John Rooke and Patrick Garvey.

In April 1981 the Orchestra's
office was the scene of a
happy but emotional reunion,
with a visit from the first
LPO managing director,
Thomas Russell (second left).
With him are three
contemporaries still in the
Orchestra – Valentine
Kennedy (left), John Kuchmy
and Wrayburn Glasspool
(third and fourth left) – and
Stephen Crabtree.

Amid the deep snow of Christmas week 1981, the West German Chancellor Helmut Schmidt flew to London for a very special assignment. Together with pianists Christoph Eschenbach and Justuz Frantz he took the third part in Mozart's *Concerto for Three Pianos*.

All three are seen here recording the work at EMI's Abbey Road Studio.

At a press conference held in London in September 1981 it was announced that Klaus Tennstedt would take over from Sir Georg Solti as Principal Conductor. It was the first time that the two maestros had met.

Postscript

by Stephen Crabtree, Managing Director,
London Philharmonic Orchestra Limited

This has been a celebration of the London Philharmonic Orchestra, a record of fifty illustrious years of music-making. Such a story would seem to provide reasonable grounds for optimism. It would be wrong, however, not to recognize that the immediate future holds problems as great as any that have occurred in the past, even during those bleak days of war.

While acknowledging with gratitude the financial support we receive from the Arts Council and the Greater London Council, through the London Orchestral Concert Board, and recording also our great debt to Lambert and Butler, Commercial Union Assurance, Pioneer High Fidelity, Marks and Spencer and Courage for their sponsorship and encouragement, particularly in these times of cutback and recession, we must emphasize that the Orchestra's continued existence involves walking an economic tightrope from which other bodies have recently fallen. It is not conducive to artistic creativity if the peace of mind of the musicians is constantly distracted by monetary cares and the stresses of an overcrowded programme.

One important stabilizing factor in this respect must be for the Orchestra to have a permanent home, not only to foster links between us and our public, but also to give the company a sense of artistic identity in place of its current nomadic state.

We must also face up to the artistic challenge of the eighties and after, denying any idea that we are a museum culture, but rather seeking to broaden our base, to bring the widest range of musical experience to the widest number of people, attracting and educating new audiences, especially of young people.

There is ever a danger that, through misunderstanding or through pressure of work in their different spheres, a gulf may develop between the orchestral players and the outside world. We must bridge any gap between the Orchestra and its public by all means possible.

Writing forty years ago, my predecessor Thomas Russell ended his book *Philharmonic* with a paragraph which still applies today:

If our musical future has been never more promising, it has been never more in danger. We must build and build, preserve what we have inherited and establish it upon a foundation that will withstand the unimagined shocks to come, upon a foundation not of stone but of strong roots, the roots of a tree which may bend and shake, but which will endure and spread its branches, giving shelter and refreshment to humanity throughout the ages.

June 1982

Behind the scenes is a small staff, employed by the players, to handle the day to day running of the orchestra. Based at the LPO's office at 53 Welbeck Street, the administration is constantly involved with booking artists, halls, rehearsal times, recording sessions, planning tours, designing and printing posters, programmes books and so on and generally coping with the complex problems of orchestral management.

ADMINISTRATION

MANAGING DIRECTOR
Stephen Crabtree

Personal Assistant
Jacqueline Noltingk

CONCERTS MANAGER
Rosalie Cody

Secretary, and London Philharmonic Society Membership Secretary
Shirley Whitfield

TOURS/SEASONAL ENGAGEMENTS MANAGER
and Assistant Company Secretary
Jean Stephenson

ACCOUNTANT
Christopher Wheeler-Grix

Assistant
Ann Cox

PUBLICITY AND PUBLIC RELATIONS
Rosalind Freeborn (*Publicity Manager*)
Eric Mason
Gillian Pole

CLASSICS FOR PLEASURE CONCERTS ORGANISER
Rowena Unsworth

RECEPTIONIST AND TELEPHONIST
Kay Foley

PERSONNEL MANAGER
Peter Chrippes

LIBRARIAN
Allan Fry

Assistant
Clare Bowler-Green

STAGE MANAGER
Kenneth Graham

Assistant
Vic Murphy

JUBILEE COMMITTEE OF HONOUR

Chairman Sir Francis Sandilands, CBE

The Lord Annan, OBE
Mrs Ian Anstruther
Sir John Barnes, KCMG, MBE
Sir Isaiah Berlin, OM, CBE, FBA, MA
Sir John Betjeman, CBE, CLit.
Nigel Broackes
Sir Alan Campbell, GCMG
George Christie
John Craig
Raphael Djanogly, JP, OSt.J
The Rt Rev and Rt Hon Gerald Ellison, KCVO
The Lord Gibson
Sir Peter Hall, CBE
The Rt Hon Earl Jellicoe, DSO, MC
Sir Claus Moser, KCB, CBE, FBA
John Raisman
The Lord Reilly
Philip Shelbourne
The Rt Hon The Lord Thomson of Monifieth, KT
Sir Charles Troughton, CBE, MC, TD
Sir Huw Wheldon, OBE, MC, LLD, DLitt.
Sir David Willcocks, CBE, MC

LPO COUNCIL

Chairman Victor Head
Secretary Stephen Crabtree

Mrs J. Aubrey Jones
Sir Adrian Boult, CH
Nicholas Busch
Moran Caplat, CBE
Dr John Creightmore
John Denison, CBE
Paul Gillham
Mrs B. Rosenfeld
Francis Sitwell
Sir Georg Solti, KBE
Lady Solti
Cyril Spencer
Mrs J. Steinberg
John Ward
Laurence Watt
Patrick Wiener

Michael Kaye *(GLC)*
George Mann, OBE *(LOCB)*
Eric Thompson, OBE *(Arts Council)*

Hutchinson & Co. (Publishers) Ltd

An imprint of the Hutchinson Publishing Group
17–21 Conway Street, London W1P 6JD

Hutchinson Group (Australia) Pty Ltd
30–32 Cremorne Street, Richmond South, Victoria 3121
PO Box 151, Broadway, New South Wales 2007

Hutchinson Group (NZ) Ltd
32–34 View Road, PO Box 40–086, Glenfield, Auckland 10

Hutchinson Group (SA) Pty Ltd
PO Box 337, Bergvlei 2012, South Africa

First published 1982
© London Philharmonic Orchestra Limited 1982

Photoset in Plantin by V & M Graphics Ltd, Aylesbury, Bucks

Printed in Great Britain.

ISBN 0 09 147300 4

Designed by Roger Walker

ACKNOWLEDGEMENTS

The author and publishers wish to thank the following for permission to reproduce photographs:

Arup Associates, pages 84 *above*, 85
Clive Barda, 70 *above*
Barratts Photo Press, 55 *above and below*
BBC Hulton Picture Library, 37 *above and below*
BBC Stills Library, 27 *centre*, 42 *below*, 49 *below*, 73
Bernard & Kruks, 50 *left*
Colin Busby, 69 *above and below*, 71 *above and below*,
72 *above and below*, 79 *above and below*,
80 *centre and below*, 81, 84 *centre*, 86 *above*,
centre and below, 91 *above and below*, 92,
94 *above and below*, 98 *above*, 99, 100 *below*,
101 *above and below*, 102, 103 *above*,
centre and below
Camera Press, 6 (photograph by Snowdon)
Central Office of Information, 46 *below*,
47 *above and below*, 50–51 *below centre*
EMI, 97, 106, 107, 108 *above and below*
Fox Photos, 20 *above*, 56
W. H. R. Godwin, 96 *above*
The Gramophone Company, 14 *below*
Guy Gravett, 95 *below*
Grimsby Evening Telegraph, 63 *above*

Illustrated London News, 68 *below*
International News Photos, page 24 *above*
Michael Jarrett, 104 *above*
Clifford Lake, 27 *centre*, 28 *below*
LCC, Parks Department, 62
Leicester Mercury, 14–15 *centre*
Allan McDougall, 31 *above*
Munich Pressefoto, 42 *above*
Pictorial press, 21 *below*
Punjab Photo Service, 65 *above*
Henry Ramage, 52 *below*, 53 *below*
Rank Organisation, 57
Alf Reynolds, 63 *below*
Stuart Robinson, 85 *below*, 104 *below*
Thomas Russell, 50–51 *above centre and centre*
Roger Taylor, 93
Wakefield Express Series, 54 *right*
Alex Wilson, 87 *above and below*
Youth & Music (photograph by Roger Holmes), 98 *below*

All other photographs are courtesy of
the London Philharmonic Orchestra Archives.

NOTES

1 Quoted in Thomas Russell, *Philharmonic Decade* (Hutchinson & Co., Ltd, 1944), pp. 18–19.
2 Ibid., p. 34.
3 Ibid., p. 40.
4 Ibid., p. 42.
5 Ibid., p. 43.
6 Ibid., p. 54.
7 Berta Geissmar, *The Baton and the Jackboot* (Hamish Hamilton, 1944), p. 357.
8 Russell, pp. 63–4.
9 Ibid., p. 85.
10 Ibid., p. 75.
11 Ibid., p. 88.
12 Ibid., p. 90.
13 Ibid., p. 90.
14 Geissmar, p. 387.
15 Russell, p. 97.
16 Ibid., p. 97.
17 Ibid., pp. 97–8.
18 Ibid., pp. 105–6.
19 Ibid., pp. 107–8.
20 Ibid., p. 105.
21 Ursula Vaughan Williams, *R. V. W.: A biography of Ralph Vaughan Williams* (Oxford University Press, 1964), p. 341.
22 Sir Adrian Boult, *My Own Trumpet* (Hamish Hamilton, 1973), p. 159.
23 Sleeve note for EMI records SLS5209.